MW00747807

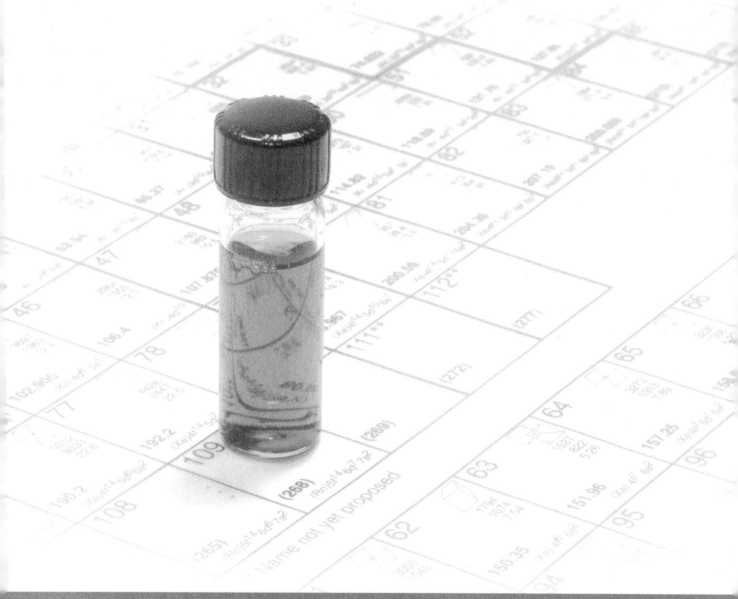

ELEMENTS OF FAITH

Faith Facts and Learning
Lessons from the Periodic Table

Richard D. Duncan

Elements of Faith

First Printing: September 2008

Copyright © 2008 Richard D. Duncan. All rights reserved. No part of this book may be used or reproduced in any manner whatsoever without written permission of the publisher, except in the case of brief quotations in articles and reviews. For information, write Master Books Inc., P.O. Box 726, Green Forest, AR 72638.

ISBN-13: 978-0-89051-547-1
ISBN-10: 0-89051-547-6
Library of Congress Number: 2008935773

Cover design by Diana Bogardus.
Interior design by Diana Bogardus & Rebekah Krall.

All photos from Shutterstock.com, istock.com, or photos.com unless otherwise noted.

Unless otherwise noted, all Scripture is from the New King James Version.

Printed in the USA.

Please visit our website for other great titles: www.masterbooks.net.

For information regarding author interviews, please contact the publicity department at (870) 438-5288.

ELEMENTS OF FAITH

Faith Facts and Learning
Lessons from the Periodic Table

Richard D. Duncan

Dedicated to:

To Scott and Rick, my pastors, for inspiration and teaching,
 to Carolyn for love and support,
 and to Jeff for wise advice.

*"As iron sharpens iron, so a man sharpens
the countenance of his friend."* —*Proverbs 27:17*

Table of Contents

HYDROGEN: "Forming Water"

"And the Spirit of God moved upon the face of the waters." (Gen. 1:2)

DATA

> Hydrogen is the most abundant element in the universe, making up over 90 percent of it.

> It was discovered in 1766 by the English chemist Henry Cavendish, who later (1781) showed that water was formed by the combustion of hydrogen in air.

> The word hydrogen comes from two Greek words: *hydros* and *genes,* meaning "water forming."

> As a gas, hydrogen is a diatomic molecule with the formula H•H or H_2.

> The formula for water is H_2O.

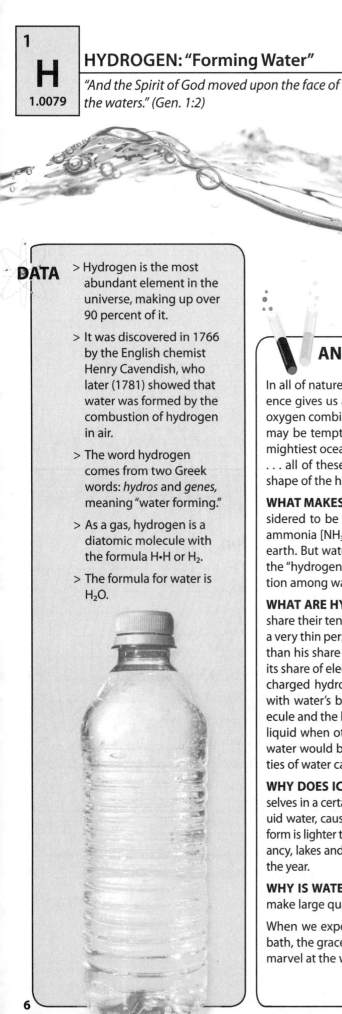

ANALYSIS

In all of nature, there is nothing quite so beautiful and yet so simple as water. Science gives us a special appreciation for it. Two tiny hydrogen atoms and a single oxygen combine to form the most abundant compound on earth, so common we may be tempted to take it for granted. From a delicate crystal snowflake to the mightiest ocean wave . . . from the clouds of a blazing sunset to a raging waterfall . . . all of these wonders of creation owe their beauty to the unique boomerang shape of the humble little molecule, H_2O.

WHAT MAKES WATER UNIQUE? Water, made up of just three small atoms, is considered to be a "light" molecule. Most molecules of similar size (methane [CH_4], ammonia [NH_3], carbon dioxide [CO_2], etc.) are gasses at normal temperatures on earth. But water is a liquid. Why? It is largely due to a phenomenon scientists call the "hydrogen bond," although it is hardly a bond at all. It is just a fleeting attraction among water molecules as they pass each other.

WHAT ARE HYDROGEN BONDS? Although the three atoms in a water molecule share their ten electrons, that sharing is not equal. It is like a very large person and a very thin person sharing a bed on a cold night; the larger one is likely to get more than his share of the blanket. Likewise, in H_2O, the oxygen atom "hogs" more than its share of electrons, giving it a slight negative charge and leaving each positively charged hydrogen nucleus partially exposed. This distribution of charge, along with water's boomerang shape, causes a "tug" between the oxygen in one molecule and the hydrogen in another. This causes water to stick together and remain liquid when other light molecules would evaporate. Without hydrogen bonding, water would boil away at about 150°F below zero! This and other unique properties of water caused by hydrogen bonding allow life to exist.

WHY DOES ICE FLOAT? Hydrogen bonds cause water molecules to arrange themselves in a certain way as the temperature nears freezing, making ice lighter than liquid water, causing it to float. (Water is one of the few substances in which the solid form is lighter than the liquid; another is Bismuth, element no. 83.) Without ice's buoyancy, lakes and rivers in cold climates would freeze solid and remain frozen much of the year.

WHY IS WATER BLUE? Hydrogen bonds absorb certain wavelengths of light to make large quantities of water appear blue.

When we experience the coolness of a drink of water or the comfort of a warm bath, the graceful waves of the sea or the beauty of a sunset, let us never cease to marvel at the wisdom of our Maker, the Creator of the hydrogen bond.

REACTION: *LIVING WATER*

Today we have many varieties of water to choose from: bottled water, tap water, mineral water, softened water, imported water, and more. But there is a type of water that will never be bought or sold: living water.

When Jesus met a woman at a well in Samaria, He told her that His followers would receive "living water" that would give them eternal life. He said ". . . whoever drinks of this water [Greek: *hydros*] will thirst again, but whoever drinks of the water that I shall give him will never thirst. But the water that I shall give him will become in him a fountain of water springing up into everlasting life" (John 4:10–14).

Later John explains (in John 7:39) that living water is actually the Holy Spirit, the same Spirit that moved upon "the face of the waters" in Genesis 1:2. And at the other end of the Bible, in Revelation, we read that living water is free and available to all, when Jesus invites us to . . .

"Come. And let him that is athirst come. And whosoever will, let him take the water of life freely" (Rev. 22:17; KJV).

Just as physical water is needed for biological life, "living water" is vital for our life and growth as Christians. No athlete can compete without consuming enough water, and we cannot expect to grow and prosper in our Christian lives unless we have a healthy amount of the "water of life" in our spiritual diets. All we have to do is ask.

1. What force causes water molecules to be attracted to each other?

   a. gravity   b. magnetism   c. hydrogen bonding   d. diffusion

2. Which of the following best describes the shape of a water molecule?

   a. cross   b. barbell   c. boomerang   d. triangle

3. TRUE or FALSE: The hydrogen and oxygen atoms in a water molecule share their electrons equally.

4. The Greek word for "water" is _____. (Fill in the blank.)

5. Hydrogen makes up more than _____ percent of the universe.

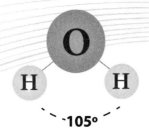

The water molecule is shaped like a boomerang.

RESPONSE

"Heavenly Father, thank You for the beauty of our created world. Thank You for the enjoyment we can receive from even the simplest of Your gifts, water itself.

"Give me the gift of living water, so that my soul will be satisfied, and so that I will have the strength each day to do the work You have set before me. Amen."

2	
He	
4.0026	

HELIUM: "From the Sun"

"Then the righteous will shine forth as the sun (Greek: helios) in the kingdom of their Father. He who has ears to hear, let him hear!" (Matt. 13:43).

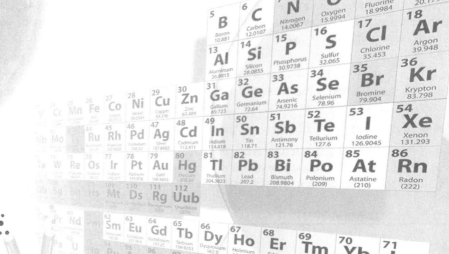

DATA

> In 1868, when French astronomer Pierre Janssen studied the spectrum of sunlight through a prism, he noticed the spectral line of an unknown element that he presumed was a metal. He named it "helium," from the Greek word *helios* meaning "sun." The "-ium" ending indicated his belief that it was a metal.

> In 1895 Scottish chemist Sir William Ramsey found a previously undiscovered gas on earth with the same spectrum as Jannsen's "metal," proving that helium was actually a gas.

> Helium is the only element ending with "-ium" that is a nonmetal.

> Helium is believed to form in the sun by the fusion of hydrogen nuclei.

ANALYSIS

The name of the gas helium comes from the Greek word *helios,* meaning "the sun." Helios was also the name of the Greek sun god.

Like many pagans of Bible times, the Greeks and Romans worshiped the sun. They believed that the sun was a blazing chariot that the god Helios drove across the sky every day. In one of their many sun myths, Phaethon, the son of Helios, stole his father's sun chariot and went on a tragic joyride. The boy could not control the chariot and nearly caused heaven and earth to be burned up (in the process creating the Sahara Desert!). Zeus, the king of the gods, was forced to kill Phaethon with a bolt of lightning to end his wild ride.

In Egypt, a land of almost constant sun and little rain, sun worship was central to everyday life. Their sun god, Amon-Re, was born anew every morning; he grew and became strong in the heat of the day; then he faded away and died each night. They believed Amon-Re was the first king of Egypt. The center of Egyptian sun worship was the city of On, which the Greeks called Heliopolis, "City of the Sun."

Sun worship also existed in ancient India, Africa, Mesopotamia, England, and among the Maya, the Aztec, and the Inca of the Americas.

But the ancient Jews were different. As God's chosen people, they were taught that the sun was not to be worshiped. Like all other forces in the universe, the sun is a creation of Yahweh, the one true God. The Jews were not to bow down to "anything that is in heaven above or in the earth beneath" (Exod. 20:4). The sun and other heavenly bodies were created for man's benefit, not to be worshiped: to determine times and seasons (Gen. 1:14), night and day (Gen 1:5; Jer. 31:35), and the points of the compass (Is. 45:6; Ps. 50:1). The Bible tells us that the sun also serves to symbolize God's character: His watchfulness (Ps. 19:4–6), His dependability (Ps. 72:4–5), His healing (Mal. 4:2), and His protection:

"For the LORD God is a sun and shield; the LORD will give grace and glory" (Ps. 84:11).

REACTION: *TRUE AND FALSE WORSHIP*

Idol worship or idolatry is the act of worshiping something that is created (whether by man or by God) rather than the Creator. During Paul's missionary journeys into the Greek and Roman world, he found a civilization that had forgotten the true God and worshiped forces of nature, like the sun and idols created by man. "[They] exchanged the truth of God for the lie, and worshiped and served the creature [or created things] more than the Creator, who is blessed forever. Amen" (Rom. 1:25).

What is the result of this false worship? Paul says that it leads to a long list of societal and individual sins: sexual immorality, wickedness, envy, murder, strife, law breaking, etc. (Rom. 1:26–32). He paints a picture of the sinful conditions that history tells us led to the downfall of the Greek and Roman civilizations. Paul's picture is frighteningly reflective of modern society as well.

TRUE WORSHIP. False worship focuses on created (physical) things, but true worship is spiritual. Jesus said: "God is Spirit; and those who worship Him must worship in spirit and truth" (John 4:24). Worship does not depend on how well we dress or the cost of the church's sound system. It doesn't depend on a church building or choir. These things can even detract from worship when we focus on our surroundings rather than listening to God's Spirit and truly submitting ourselves to Him.

QUICK QUIZ

1. Except for helium, elements with names ending in –um or –ium are _____.

   a. gasses   b. radioactive   c. metallic   d. poisonous

2. The Greek word for "sun" is _____. (Fill in the blank)

3. A French astronomer, Pierre Janssen, discovered the existence of helium on the surface of the sun. Who discovered helium here on earth?

4. Worship of the sun or anything other than God is considered to be _____. (Fill in the blank.)

5. Which ancient culture worshiped the sun as a god?

   a. Egypt   b. Greek   c. Roman   d. All of the above

RESPONSE

"Little children, keep yourselves from idols. Amen" (1 John 5:21).

The Bible tells us to examine ourselves, to make sure that there is nothing in our lives that we place above our relationship with God. The world offers many physical temptations or idols to distract us from worshiping "in spirit and in truth." The love of money and power (Matt. 6:24), immoral entertainment (Ps. 101:2–4), and sinful desires of the flesh (1 Pet. 2:11–12) are just a few.

"Lord, help me to worship only You this day. Help me to put away all idols and anything that distracts me from true and deeper worship. And help me to remember to praise You in all things."

3
Li
6.941

LITHIUM: A Surprise Discovery in "Stone"

"He who is without sin among you, let him throw a stone [Greek: lithos] at her first" (John 8:7).

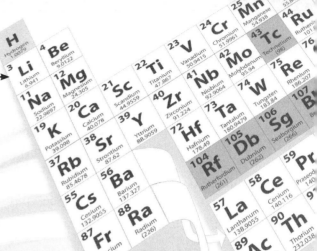

DATA

> Lithium is the lightest metal; it is soft and silvery-white in its pure form.

> Lithium is highly reactive and quickly forms a gray oxide layer when exposed to air, but it is less reactive than other alkali (Group I) metals.

> Lithium was discovered in 1817 by the Swedish chemist Johan Arfvedson.

> Arfvedson took its name from the Greek word *lithos*, meaning "stone."

ANALYSIS

In the early 1800s the brilliant British scientist Sir Humphry Davy discovered several new elements. In 1807 he discovered two more: sodium and potassium. These elements had similar characteristics, such as their appearance and the way they combined with oxygen in a certain ratio. Davy referred to these elements as "alkali metals."

In 1817 the Swedish chemist Johan Arfvedson discovered a new metallic element in a mineral found near Stockholm. His new element had properties similar to the alkali metals Davy had discovered ten years earlier. This was unexpected because Davy's alkalis were both derived from plant sources (trees for potassium and seaweed for sodium). Arfvedson was so surprised to find this new element in a mineral or rock that he named it after the Greek word, *lithos* meaning "stone."

"STONE" AND "ROCK" IN THE NEW TESTAMENT

Like English, biblical Greek had two words for stone and rock: *lithos* and *petra*.

Lithos refers to individual stones, like those common in the Holy Land. John the Baptist said that God could raise up "children of Abraham" from these stones (Matt. 3:9) and Jesus said the stones would cry out in praise if His worshippers were silenced (Luke 19:40). These were also the stones that would have been hurled at the woman caught in adultery had Jesus not rescued her (John 8:7). Sometimes the word means "building stones." When Christ called Himself "the stone the builders rejected" (Luke 20:17), *lithos* was the word He used.

On the other hand, *petra* referred to larger types of rock: foundations of buildings (the wise man's house in Matt. 7:24), outcrops of rock (Luke 8:6), or even mountains (Rev. 6:15).

In one important verse, both words are used. After Jesus was crucified, Joseph of Arimathea took Jesus' body down from the cross and ". . . laid him in a tomb which had been hewn out of the rock [*petra*], and rolled a stone [*lithos*] against the door of the tomb" (Mark 15:46).

After three days, the disciples returned to the tomb and were amazed to find that "…the stone [*lithos*] had been rolled away — for it was very large" (Mark 16:4).

Just like Johan Arfvedson, Jesus' disciples made a surprising discovery "in stone."

REACTION: *FOUNDATION*

Some of the parables, or teaching stories, of Jesus were hard to understand. However, most of them were very simple and straight-forward. For example, Jesus' parable of the wise man who "built his house upon the rock" (from Matt. 7:24–29) is so easily understood that it is used in children's Sunday school classes. Yet it carries a lot of meaning.

When you build a house, you can fill it with the finest furniture. You can paint it with beautiful colors. You can have the prettiest floors, windows, and walls. But if the foundation is weak, your house will not stand the test of time. Storms will come and the wood will rot and the floors will warp. All of your hard work will be in vain.

A person's life is a lot like a house. You may have a good education or lots of money or good looks. Your life may seem great in the good times, but tragedies and hard times, like storms, come into all of our lives. If you build your life on the foundation of Christ and His Word, it will withstand whatever comes your way. As the old song says, "On Christ the solid rock I stand. All other ground is sinking sand."

Each day of your life can also be like building a house. Reading God's Word and prayer each morning is a good way to build a firm foundation for the day ahead. If you do this, you will find that your accomplishments will be lasting (1 Cor. 3: 9–15).

QUICK QUIZ

1. Lithium is the _____ of all the metals.

    a. hardest   b. lightest   c. most dangerous   d. densest

2. What are the Greek words for the following terms?

    a. Stone (individual   b. Rock (massive, like a
         pieces of stone)   cliff or foundation)

3. Which of the disciples' name meant "rock"?

    a. Matthew   b. John   c. Judas   d. Peter

4. Lithium, sodium, and potassium are all found in the same column of the Periodic Table. Metals in this column are called _____ metals. (Fill in the blank.)

5. Every building needs to be built on a firm _____. (Fill in the blank.)

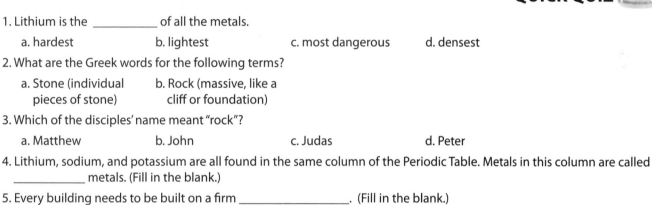

RESPONSE

"Lord, help me to be like the wise man who built his house upon the rock and not the foolish man who built on the sand. Let my life and all I have, whether it be my marriage, my job, or my children, be built on the best foundation of all — Christ, the solid rock."

4
Be
9.0122

BERYLLIUM: "A Bright & Beautiful Jewel"

"I lifted my eyes and looked, and behold, a certain man clothed in linen, whose waist was girded with gold of Uphaz! His body was like beryl, his face like the appearance of lightning, his eyes like torches of fire . . ." (Dan. 10: 5–6).

DATA

> Beryllium is named after the precious stone "beryl," in which the element was discovered. Beryl is still the ore from which most beryllium is derived.

> Beryllium was discovered in 1797 by the French chemist L.N. Vauquelin.

> Emerald, aquamarine, morganite, and heliodor are varieties of beryl in various colors.

> Beryl appears in the Old Testament as one of the gems representing the 12 Tribes of Israel (Exod. 28:17–21) and in the New Testament as one of the foundation stones representing the 12 "Apostles of the Lamb" (Rev. 21:14–21).

ANALYSIS

The prophet Daniel saw God in an intense vision (Dan. 10:4–7). He was so overwhelmed by what he saw that he passed out. When he woke up, Daniel was unable to speak for a time. When he wrote down what he had seen, he could only describe the fantastic vision in terms of the most brilliant things he knew: gold, fire, lightning, and the dazzling gem, beryl! Today geologists know beryl by its chemical formula: $Be_3Al_2Si_6O_{18}$ or "beryllium aluminum silicate."

Beryl represents God's presence.

The dazzling appearance of precious gems was used to represent God's presence elsewhere in the Bible as well. When Ezekiel had his vision of the four living creatures (actually angels), he described their appearance as being like the blazing gem beryl also (Ezek. 1:16 and 10:9).

In the New Testament, John had his own vision of heaven. He described God's appearance in terms of several precious stones: God sitting on His throne was said to be like jasper, sardius, and emerald to look upon (Rev. 4:3). (Emerald is a green variety of beryl.)

Just as precious stones represented God's presence, they can illustrate spiritual qualities as well:

PEARLS REPRESENT GOD'S KINGDOM. Christ referred to pearls twice in Matthew's Gospel. In the Sermon on the Mount, Christ compared His teachings about the Kingdom to pearls (Matt. 7:6). And in the parable of the "Pearl of Great Price," Christ compared the kingdom of heaven to a pearl merchant seeking and finding one perfect pearl and selling all that he owned to obtain it (Matt. 13:45–46), just as God the Father would give His most precious possession (His only begotten Son) to redeem you and me from our sins. And Revelation tells us that the very gates of the kingdom of heaven are made of pearl (Rev. 21:21).

RUBIES REPRESENT WISDOM. The brilliant red ruby was a highly valued stone, but as Job said, the worth of precious gems should not even be "mentioned" in the same breath as "wisdom," for its price is "above rubies" (Job 28:18). The Proverbs also tell us that rubies come in a distant second when compared to godly wisdom (Prov. 3:14–15, 8:11, and 20:15). Likewise, a virtuous wife is far more valuable than rubies (Prov. 31:10).

REACTION: *GOD'S GEMS*

The Old Testament Book of Malachi talks about two groups of people who lived during a difficult period in Israel's history. One group of Israelites was called "arrogant." They complained about keeping God's commandments. These people turned away from their faith and said, "It is useless to serve God" (Mal. 3:14).

But another group was faithful to the Lord. They met together and talked about their situation. They drew up a "Scroll of Remembrance" and committed themselves to fear and honor the name of the Lord. Malachi said that God heard the prayers of these faithful believers. God called them His "jewels" and promised that they would be spared in the difficult days to come.

"They shall be Mine," says the LORD of hosts, "on the day that I make them My jewels. And I will spare them as a man spares his own son who serves him" (Mal. 3:17).

QUICK QUIZ

1. Which of the following is not a form of the gem beryl?

    a. emerald   b. ruby   c. aquamarine   d. heliodor

2. Which chemist discovered beryllium?

    a. Davy   b. Boyle   c. Curie   d. Vauquelin

3. Beryl is the main _____ from which most beryllium is derived. (Fill in the blank.)

4. In the Bible, what gem is frequently associated with "wisdom"?

    a. ruby   b. diamond   c. emerald   d. onyx

5. In Malachi chapter 3, God speaks of His faithful followers as _____. (Fill in the blank.)

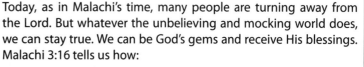

RESPONSE

Today, as in Malachi's time, many people are turning away from the Lord. But whatever the unbelieving and mocking world does, we can stay true. We can be God's gems and receive His blessings. Malachi 3:16 tells us how:

FEAR THE LORD: We must always recognize and honor God for who He is and put Him in the proper place in our lives.

SPEAK OFTEN ONE TO ANOTHER: We must be faithful and consistent in fellowship with other believers, always including the Lord in our plans and committing ourselves to Him.

THINK UPON HIS NAME: Focus on God. Spend time in prayer. And seek God's wisdom in the love letter that He left for us: the Bible.

"Heavenly Father, help me to not be affected by the unbelieving world around me. I want to fear You and honor Your Son. I want to be a shining jewel in Your kingdom. Help me to be faithful until I stand before You like Daniel and see Your face, shining as 'gold and beryl, lightning and fire.' Amen."

BORON: "The Cleanness of My Hands"

"The LORD rewarded me according to my righteousness; according to the cleanness [Hebrew: bor] of my hands He has recompensed me" (Ps. 18:20).

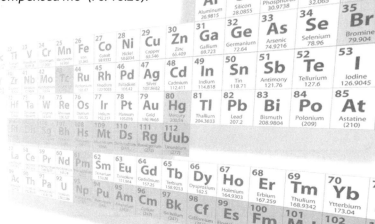

DATA

> Boron compounds have been used for thousands of years, especially "borax" ($Na_2B_4O_7$), which is used for glass-making, ceramics, and detergents.

> The English chemist Sir Humphry Davy and two French chemists (L. J. Gay-Lussac and L. J. Thenard) isolated boron from boric acid (HBO_2) at about the same time in 1808.

> The name boron is derived from borax. The "–on" ending indicates its similarity to carbon and silicon.

> The origin of the word borax is Arabic, but the root "bor-" is found in Hebrew as well. Forms of the Hebrew word appear in the Bible as "cleanness" (*bor*, as in the verse above) and "soap" (*boritz*, in Jer. 2:22 and Mal. 3:2).

ANALYSIS

Dr. Joseph Lister (1827–1912) is considered the father of modern surgery. He was responsible for many medical advances, including drainage tubes for wounds and "catgut" sutures, which dissolve in the human body. But his most important innovation was the use of "antiseptic techniques." Before the 1870s, surgeons did not wear gloves or gowns. Often they made no attempt to even clean up between surgeries. Many considered it a status symbol to be covered with blood from previous operations. As a result, about 50 percent of patients who had major surgery died from infections, often after otherwise successful operations. In the days before the discovery of germs, doctors believed that infections arose spontaneously and that there was no way to stop them.

By 1860 Lister was already a successful surgeon when he began corresponding (and a lifelong friendship) with the French chemist (and fellow Christian) Louis Pasteur. Pasteur's work had shown that the spoiling of milk and wine resulted from germs in the air. Lister concluded that such germs might also cause human infection. If so, there might be ways to prevent germs from reaching his patients. Lister began looking for ways to do just that.

Lister experimented with several chemical solutions he called "antiseptics" in his operating rooms to clean wounds and soak bandages. He even sprayed them in the air to kill bacteria before they could reach the patient. The results were remarkable. His patients had practically no infections. However, after repeated exposures, these antiseptics were harmful to Lister and the surgeons who worked with him, bleaching and numbing the skin and causing vision and breathing problems.

Lister eventually found a chemical that was very effective yet safe for medical personnel; it became a standard antiseptic in operating rooms for decades. This chemical was *boric* acid (HBO_2). Just like David in the verse quoted above, the Lord rewarded Dr. Lister according to the "cleanness (*bor*) of his hands."

Like so many of the giants in the history of science, Dr. Lister was a faithful Christian. A contemporary of Lister wrote that he was a humble servant of God who "always asked for His guidance in moments of difficulty. . . . (He) believed himself to be directly inspired by God. . . . To Lister, the operating theatre was a temple."

Note: Boric acid is still widely used in medicine. For example, it is used in eye drops to prevent eye infections.

REACTION: *CLEAN HANDS/CLEAN HEART*

In the Bible, references to the hand often have symbolic meaning. Your hands represent the "work" that you do, just as your heart represents your "thought and feelings." And to have clean hands means to resist evil and to do good things for God. Our theme verse, Psalm 18:20, says that God will reward us if we have a clean heart (righteousness) and clean hands (good works). In Psalm 24:3–4 learn that only those with clean hands and pure hearts are able to "stand in the Lord's holy place."

In the New Testament, James tells us much about the importance of "good works." "Cleanse your hands, you sinners; and purify your hearts, you double-minded" (James 4: 8–9). This idea also comes through in probably the best-known verse in James: "Faith [a clean heart] without works [clean hands] is dead" (James 2:20).

In Scripture, a person's profession is often referred to as the "work of one's hands." By cleaning his own hands, Joseph Lister revolutionized the medical profession and ultimately led to the saving of millions of lives.

QUICK QUIZ

1. Dr. Joseph Lister is considered to be the Father of Modern_____. (Fill in the blank.)

2. Boron is the main element in _____, a compound used in glass-making, ceramics, and detergents. (Fill in the blank.)

3. The Hebrew word *bor* means _____.

   a. cleanness   b. blood   c. germs   d. work

4. Dr. Joseph Lister used _____ acid as an antiseptic during surgery.

   a. hydrochloric   b. boric   c. hydrobromic   d. amino

5. Dr. Joseph Lister was friends with what great French scientist and fellow Christian?

RESPONSE

"Come into my heart, Lord, and make it clean, a place fit for You to live. Help me to keep it clean for the sake of the gospel and Your kingdom. Lord, clean my hands as well for the sake of my family and to show Your love to my fellow man. Help me to find ways to honor You in my profession and to seek Your will daily. Amen."

How can I, like Joseph Lister, honor God with the cleanliness of my hands and heart this day?

6
C
12.0107

CARBON: "Sir Humphry Davy and the Mine Safety Lamp"

"Your word is a lamp to my feet, and a light to my path" (Ps. 119:105).

DATA

> Elemental carbon has been known in three forms since antiquity: diamond, graphite, and charcoal.

> In 1772 the Frenchman Antoine Lavoisier (1743–1794) proved that all three of these forms were composed of the same element, which he called *carbone* from the French word for charcoal. In English, the word became carbon.

> Later it was learned that carbon forms the molecular backbone of all living things and is found in all organic matter.

> Combustion (C + O$_2$ → CO$_2$ + ΔH, where ΔH stands for "the release of energy") is the most basic and essential chemical reaction in biological life and human civilization.

> Anthracite, the purest form of coal, is up to 96 percent carbon.

ANALYSIS

In the 1800s the industrial revolution was well underway in England, and wood was the fuel that sustained it. But as forests dwindled due to the demands of progress, the English turned to a new energy source to heat their homes and power their factories: coal.

England had many coal deposits on the surface. But as miners dug into them, they became underground coal seams that ran for miles. New mining techniques were devised to follow the coal, which led to new dangers for miners. Many were lost due to two main factors: lack of oxygen, and mine explosions caused by high concentrations of an odorless, highly flammable gas, which they called "firedamp." Today we call it methane or natural gas (CH$_4$).

Oxygen could be monitored with canaries and other caged birds, which would succumb to low oxygen levels and warn the miners. The other danger remained for many years. Oil lamps were the only light source available at that time, and the lamp flames led to numerous deadly explosions. Eventually the nation turned to Sir Humphry Davy (1778–1829), the brilliant chemist who had already isolated several elements. They asked Davy to develop a light source that could be used safely in the mines.

Davy created an oil lamp with a wire screen mesh that covered the flame. The mesh spread out the heat of the flame and reduced the flame temperature to a level beneath the ignition point of natural gas. Davy's invention reduced the loss of life dramatically and increased his already great popularity. It came to be known as the "mine safety lamp" or simply "Davy's Lamp."

Davy's Lamp quickly became the industry standard and was used all over the world. Despite its great success, Davy had no interest is profiting from his invention. In 1816, in response to a friend who suggested that he patent it, Davy wrote, "No, my good friend, I never thought of such a thing; my sole object was to serve the cause of humanity, and if I succeeded I am amply rewarded in the gratifying of having done so." Sir Humphry Davy was a Bible-believing Christian, whose invention of the mine safety lamp was just one example of service to his fellow man.

REACTION: *THE COMBUSTION REACTION (C + O$_2$ → CO$_2$ + ENERGY)*

Combustion, the oxidation of carbon in any of its forms to produce energy and carbon dioxide, is probably the most basic and vital chemical reaction that has ever taken place. The energy that results from combustion powers civilization and even life itself. Of course, the product of the reaction CO$_2$ is much more than just an unwanted pollutant. It is the raw material needed by every green plant to grow and reproduce, from the largest sequoia to the tiniest plankton in the sea.

Mankind has utilized almost every form of organic matter (carbon) as fuel to produce thermal energy (heat) and light energy. In Bible times, burning wood, dried brush and grass, and even animal dung (depending on a person's affluence) provided heat. The story of Davy's safety lamp refers to four fuel sources: wood, coal, whale oil (in the miners' lamps), and "firedamp" (natural gas). Petroleum, coal, and natural gas provide the vast majority of energy in the modern world.

"Cellular respiration" is a special case of the combustion reaction in which "food" is the carbon source; it is a biochemical reaction that takes place on a cellular level to provide life energy for all living things.

QUICK QUIZ

1. What historical event caused a great demand for coal in 19th-century England?

2. Nineteenth-Century coal miners often encountered a dangerous gas, which they called "firedamp." The gas was colorless, odorless, and explosive. Today we call it natural gas or _____. Its chemical formula is CH$_4$. (Fill in the blank.)

3. Diamonds, graphite, and charcoal are all forms of elemental _____.

    a. coal   b. carbon   c. jewels   d. metals

4. What British scientist invented the famous "mine safety lamp" to protect coal miners?

    a. Davy   b. Lister   c. Newton   d. Pasteur

5. In Psalm 18:28, David said that God's Word is _____

    a. a heavy burden   b. like lightning   c. a lump of coal   d. lamp to my feet

RESPONSE

"For You are my lamp, O LORD; the LORD shall enlighten my darkness" (2 Sam. 22:29).

Lamps in the Bible burned olive oil and were the primary light source for homes and public buildings like the temple. Some lamps were portable and were used like lanterns. Lamps were also used in celebrations, as in Jesus' parable of "the wise and foolish virgins" (Matt. 25:1–13).

A miner in Humphry Davy's day had a special appreciation for his lamp:

> Like the "five wise virgins," a miner had to make sure to have enough oil to last in his dark environment.

> David described God's Word as "a lamp to my feet" (Ps. 119:105), and Peter called it a "light [lamp] that shines in a dark place" (2 Peter 1:19), reminding us of the miner's need to "light his path" in the dark mineshaft.

> Isaiah 62:1 tells us that "salvation [is] a lamp that burns." To the miner who benefited from Davy's lamp, having a safe light that would not ignite the dangerous gasses around him was a type of "salvation" indeed.

"Heavenly Father, thank You for being my lamp and helping me to find my way in this world. Like a miner with an important job to do in a dangerous environment, You have sent me into a dark world to share the light of the gospel with others. Help me to learn the lessons You have for me in Your Word. Amen."

7	
N	
14.0067	

NITROGEN: "The Three-fold Cord"

"Though one may be overpowered by another, two can withstand him. And a threefold cord is not quickly broken" (Eccles. 4:12).

DATA

> Nitrogen makes up 78.1 percent of the earth's atmosphere.

> Like all other elemental gasses (except the noble gasses), nitrogen occurs as a diatomic molecule N_2. However, the nitrogen atoms are connected by a triple bond ($N\equiv N$). This powerful bond makes nitrogen an extremely inert gas.

> Nitrogen was discovered in 1772 by the English chemist Daniel Rutherford.

> Nitrogen means "niter forming." Niter is an old name for saltpeter or potassium nitrate (KNO_3).

ANALYSIS

Nitrogen (N_2) makes up nearly four-fifth's of the earth's atmosphere. It is vitally important for all life, yet atmospheric nitrogen is useless to plants and animals (at least directly) due to its powerful triple bond.

Animals can break apart the double bonds of oxygen (O_2 or $O=O$) with the help of the hemoglobin molecule in their blood. Green plants use the chlorophyll molecule to overcome both the double bonds of oxygen in "respiration" and of carbon dioxide (CO_2 or $O=C=O$) in "photosynthesis." But neither animals nor plants can break down the triple bond of nitrogen (N_2 or $N\equiv N$).

Yet all living things need nitrogen; it is found in proteins, nucleic acids, vitamins, and many other organic chemicals. Since its ultimate source is the atmosphere, how does nitrogen enter our food supply? What force has the power to break its triple bond? Actually, God has provided two forces in nature to do just that.

1. LIGHTNING. Electrical storms split nitrogen molecules in the atmosphere into individual atoms. These free nitrogen atoms then quickly react with oxygen to form nitrogen dioxide (NO_2) which falls to earth dissolved in rain. Plants are able to absorb this diluted NO_2 through their roots and use it to form amino acids and proteins. However, lightning is not a reliable source for usable forms of nitrogen, so the Creator in His wisdom has provided another means.

2. NITROGEN-FIXING BACTERIA. These bacteria grow in tiny nodules on the roots of plants called legumes, which provide a stable environment for the bacteria. In return, the bacteria provide a generous supply of nitrogen in the form of ammonia (NH_3) to the plant. Exactly how these tiny bacteria are able to break nitrogen's triple bond is still a mystery to science, but all human and animal life on earth depend on this symbiotic phenomenon.

Legumes include plants whose seeds grow in pods (beans, peas, peanuts, etc.) and forage crops (like clover and alfalfa). Farmers grow legumes in rotation with other crops to ensure that sufficient nitrogen gets into the soil. Legumes provide high-quality proteins and are an important part of a healthy diet. So when you're eating your vegetables, keep in mind God's providence and His tiny little helpers, the nitrogen-fixing bacteria.

REACTION: *SPIRITUAL BONDS*

Ecclesiastes 4:12 tells us that a "three-fold cord is not quickly broken."

The Bible also speaks of other "triple bonds." These are spiritual bonds that unite believers when we act in accordance with God's Word. Jesus told His disciples in Matthew 18:19, "If two of you agree on earth concerning anything . . . it will be done for them by My Father in heaven . . ." because "where two or three are gathered together in My name, I am there in the midst of them" (verse 20). This is a wonderful promise to us as Christians. Even just two believers, united in prayer and God's will, have a special bond with Christ.

In the marriage of two Christians, this is especially true. The Bible says that a husband and wife join together as "one flesh" in the eyes of God and become "members of His [Christ's] body, of His flesh and of His bones" (Eph. 5:30–32). Marriage has often been described as a triangle with the husband and wife at the bottom corners and Jesus Christ at the top. As each spouse draws closer to Jesus through prayer and obedience, they also grow closer to each other.

QUICK QUIZ

1. Nitrogen makes up _____ of the earth's atmosphere.

    a. most   b. about half   c. a small portion   d. hardly any

2. Like oxygen, hydrogen, and the halogen gasses, nitrogen is a diatomic molecule; but unlike these gasses, the nitrogen molecule is held together by a powerful_____ bond.

    a. hydrogen   b. ionic   c. triple   d. magnetic

3. Most of the nitrogen found in the soil is produced by what type of life-form?

4. What type of plants are associated with "nitrogen fixation" in the soil?

5. Which of the following nutrients contains nitrogen?

    a. sugar   b. protein   c. carbohydrate   d. fat

RESPONSE

How tragic it is to neglect the blessings of Christian unity — whether in a church or in a marriage! On the other hand, what a blessing it is to know that when we join with a brother or sister in Christ for help in facing the difficulties and challenges in life, we can be assured of the loving presence of our Savior!

"Lord, thank You for reminding me of Your presence. Thank You for Your Holy Spirit that binds us together through all the trials and triumphs of life."

8		
O		
15.9994		

OXYGEN: "The Breath of Life"

"And the LORD God formed man of the dust of the ground, and breathed into his nostrils the breath of life; and man became a living being" (Gen. 2:7).

DATA

> Oxygen makes up about 21 percent of the volume of the air, occurring mostly as O_2.

> The name is from two Greek words: *oxy* and *genes* meaning, "acid forming" (because many acids are oxygen compounds).

> Many experts who study the history of science now give the credit for the discovery of oxygen to three famous chemists from three different countries: Joseph Priestley (1733–1804) of England, Carl Wilhelm Scheele (1742–86) of Sweden, and Antoine Lavoisier (1743–94) of France. All of them had discovered oxygen in the early 1770s.

> Priestley was the first to publish his discovery in 1774.

ANALYSIS

The Hebrew word for "breath" in the verse above is *ruach*, which is often translated as "spirit" elsewhere in the Old Testament. In this verse, God breathes "life" into Adam through his nostrils and into his lungs. The Bible makes it clear in many other verses that a man's life "is in his breath" and his breath comes from God (Job 12:10; Ezek. 37:5; Ps. 146:4; Acts 17:25; etc.).

Genesis 1:2 tells us that God's "spirit" or breath (*ruach* again) "moved upon the face of the waters" during creation. This verse seems to describe God's activity of breathing life into our world (by creating the proper mixture of oxygen and other gasses in our atmosphere) just as He breathed life into Adam's nostrils.

THE DELICATE BALANCE. As astronomers have advanced in their ability to study other planets and their moons, it has become clear that oxygen (O_2) is a rare substance in the universe, found only in traces in the rest of our solar system. But on earth it exists in abundance. Most importantly, it is found in just the right proportion: 21 percent of our atmosphere.

If the oxygen content were, say, 16 percent instead of 21 percent, life at sea level would compare to trying to breathe at the top of a mountain two miles high. Elevations higher than sea level would be largely uninhabitable by humans. Low oxygen levels would also reduce the protective ozone (O_3) layer in the upper atmosphere, allowing harmful ultraviolet rays to reach the surface.

On the other hand, higher oxygen levels would have serious consequences as well. If the concentration were 30 percent, then oxidation would occur 50 percent more rapidly, and forest fires would rage across continents. All organic matter would be highly flammable.

Other gases in our atmosphere exist in just the right levels, too. For example, carbon dioxide (CO_2) constitutes a mere 0.03 percent of our air, but its function as a so-called greenhouse gas is essential to keeping the earth at a habitable temperature. CO_2 levels also help to keep a proper pH balance in our oceans and cause plants to grow at the proper rate.

These facts and many others about our atmosphere confirm the biblical statement that on the day God "breathed" our earthly atmosphere into existence (Gen. 1:1), it was truly "very good."

REACTION: *SPIRIT*

In the Book of John, we find a story of Jesus that reminds us very much of what God did in Genesis 1:2 and 2:7: conveying life through His own breath.

Immediately after the Crucifixion, the disciples were scared, lonely, and in hiding. They were afraid that at any time the authorities who had killed Jesus would come and take them away as well. Their rabbi, friend, and spiritual leader was gone. They had lost hope.

It was at this lowest of low points that Jesus appeared to them in the flesh. He said:

"Peace to you! As the Father has sent Me, I also send you." And when He had said this, He breathed on them, and said to them, "Receive the Holy Spirit" (John 20:21–22).

Just as in the beginning when God breathed life into the world and into Adam's nostrils, Jesus Christ "breathed" life (the Holy Spirit) into His church. That life continues today in every believer.

As the old hymn says: "Breathe on me, Breath of God. Fill me with life anew, that I may love what Thou dost love, and do what Thou wouldst do."

QUICK QUIZ

1. Earth's atmosphere is _____ oxygen.

    a. 7 percent   b. 14 percent   c. 21 percent   d. 42 percent

2. The Hebrew word *ruach* means "spirit" or _____.

    a. strength   b. anger   c. light   d. breath

3. Triatomic oxygen or O_3 is an unstable, more reactive form of oxygen, also known as _____. (Fill in the blank.)

4. TRUE or FALSE: Oxygen was discovered about the same time by three different chemists in three different countries.

5. If the oxygen content of the earth's atmosphere were significantly less, human life would be impossible at_____.

    a. sea level   b. high elevations   c. low temperatures   d. the equator

RESPONSE

"God, who made the world and everything in it . . . gives to all life, BREATH, and all things" (Acts 17:24–25).

"Lord, thank You for reminding us of Your love and providence, with even the air that we breathe. Just as You breathed life into the world on its first day and into Adam on his first day, give me Your Holy Spirit today and every day, so that I will be able to serve You. Amen."

9
F
18.9984

FLUORINE: "The Modern Element"

"But you, Daniel, shut up the words, and seal the book until the time of the end; many will run to and fro, and knowledge shall increase" (Dan. 12:4).

DATA

> From the Latin *fluo*, meaning "to flow," fluorine is a pale yellow, poisonous, and highly corrosive gas. Fluorine gas is diatomic (F_2).

> Pure fluorine is very dangerous to use without proper safeguards. Many scientists died trying to isolate pure fluorine in the 19th century. These men were referred to as "Fluorine Martyrs."

> Fluorine was first successfully isolated by French chemist Henri Moissan in 1886.

> Fluorine was not produced in significant quantities until WWII and the Manhattan Project.

> Fluorine is the most reactive of all the elements, combining with every other element except two (the noble gasses—helium and neon).

> Fluorine is a member of the halogen family of elements (Group 17).

ANALYSIS

This study will consider some of the advances in technology ("increase in knowledge") prophesied in Daniel 12:4, which were made possible by fluorine chemistry.

Fluorine has the maximum number of "free" electrons in its outer electron shell: seven. But fluorine has only a tiny nucleus (nine protons) to hold onto its "hungry" electrons. This proton/electron arrangement makes fluorine the most reactive element. As a result, pure fluorine (F_2) is an extremely dangerous gas, and fluorine was one of the last of the common elements to be isolated. Yet in the 20th century, fluorine was the key to many amazing developments, which have truly changed our world.

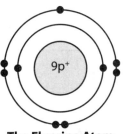

The Fluorine Atom

NUCLEAR ENERGY: The production of nuclear power depends on the separation of two isotopes of uranium, U-235 and U-238. Fluorine combines with uranium to form uranium hexafluoride (UF_6). Because of fluorine's light weight, UF_6 can be made into a gas at fairly low temperatures, and the UF_6 molecules can be separated due to the differing masses of the isotopes. Advances in fluorine chemistry made nuclear energy (and nuclear weapons) possible.

FREON: In the 1920s refrigeration was rare, expensive, and dangerous. It required the use of hazardous compounds like sulfur dioxide (SO_2) or ammonia (NH_4), which often led to disaster, such as a refrigerant leak in 1929 that killed over 100 people at a Cleveland hospital. Then Thomas Midgely, an Ohio inventor, discovered that fluorine combines with carbon and chlorine to form very stable, non-toxic compounds called chloro-fluoro-carbons or CFCs (also known as Freon). With ideal thermal properties, low cost, and ease of use, Midgely's discovery made refrigeration and air conditioning affordable and safe, and truly made the world a better place to live.

TEFLON: The long-chain fluorocarbon Teflon has the lowest known coefficient of friction of any solid and a high degree of chemical inertness. These properties make it invaluable for many applications: manufacturing, transportation, construction, aerospace . . . and probably your kitchen.

THE FUTURE: Fluorine's ability to replace hydrogen in almost any organic molecule means that, in the 21st century, the growing field of fluorocarbon chemistry will likely produce many new fluorine-based chemicals with benefits we cannot yet imagine.

REACTION: RESPONSIBILITY

The breakneck pace of technological advances reminds us of Daniel's prophecy of a time when "many will run to and fro" (increase in travel) and "knowledge shall increase" (technology). We have certainly seen both. Throughout most of human history, a man could only travel as fast as a fast horse could carry him, and most people lived and died within a short distance from where they were born. Technology has changed all that.

But as Adam and Eve learned in the Garden (Gen. 2:16–17), an "increase in knowledge" is not always a good thing. It may come at great cost. So it is with fluorine.

Chlorofluorocarbons like Freon have greatly improved our lives: our homes can be cool even in the hottest climates; we can safely store and transport foods; we can even take this cool comfort with us as we travel. But the overuse of Freon is now said to threaten the earth's ozone layer. (Today, Freon has been largely replaced with modified fluorine-based chemicals which are believed to have less of an effect on ozone.)

Likewise, thanks to fluorine, nuclear technology with its promise of inexpensive electrical energy is also a threat as rogue nations seek their own nuclear weapons. As you can see, fluorine's reactive nature makes it a double-edged sword that can be used for good or evil.

QUICK QUIZ

1. Fluorine is needed for which of these modern inventions?

   a. Freon   b. Teflon   c. modern air conditioning   d. all of the above

2. Fluorine is the most _____ of all the elements. (Fill in the blank.)

3. Production of fuel for nuclear reactors is dependent on the chemical compound called _____ hexafluoride.

   a. oxygen   b. uranium   c. silicon   d. iron

4. Fluorine is a member of what "family" of elements?

5. Early scientists who died trying to isolate fluorine were called "fluorine _____." (Fill in the blank.)

RESPONSE

The Bible tells us that God made man to have dominion over the earth (Gen. 1:28, "to fill the earth and subdue it") but also to care for it responsibly (Gen. 2:15, "to tend and keep it"). As technology becomes more powerful, engineers and scientists have a responsibility to ensure that future generations benefit, rather than suffer, from these advances . . . "until the time of the end" (Dan. 12:4).

"Heavenly Father, thank You for the blessings of chemistry and other forms of technology. Help us to use them to benefit mankind and to be mindful of the awesome consequences of using technology carelessly. Amen."

10
Ne
20.1797

NEON: "Let Your Light Shine"

"Let your light so shine before men, that they may see your good works and glorify your Father in heaven" (Matt. 5:16).

								2 He Helium 4.0026
		5 B Boron 10.881	6 C Carbon 12.0107	7 N Nitrogen 14.0067	8 O Oxygen 15.9994	9 F Fluorine 18.9984	10 Ne Neon 20.1797	

13 Al Aluminum 26.9815 | 14 Si Silicon 28.0855 | 15 P Phosphorus 30.9738 | 16 S Sulfur 32.065 | 17 Cl Chlorine 35.453 | 18 Ar Argon 39.948

31 Ga Gallium 69.723 | 32 Ge Germanium 72.64 | 33 As Arsenic 74.9216 | 34 Se Selenium 78.96 | 35 Br Bromine 79.904 | 36 Kr Krypton 83.798

49 In Indium 114.818 | 50 Sn Tin 118.71 | 51 Sb Antimony 121.76 | 52 Te Tellurium 127.6 | 53 I Iodine 126.9045 | 54 Xe Xenon 131.293

81 Tl Thallium 204.3833 | 82 Pb Lead 207.2 | 83 Bi Bismuth 208.9804 | 84 Po Polonium (209) | 85 At Astatine (210) | 86 Rn Radon (222)

DATA

> Neon is a noble gas found in minute quantities in the atmosphere (1 part per 65,000).

> It was discovered in 1898 by the English chemist Sir William Ramsey. He had been trying to isolate the gas since 1894, when he discovered argon (element no. 18).

> The element's name (from the Greek *neos*, meaning "new") was suggested by Ramsey's 13-year old son, Willie, since Ramsey was seeking a "new" noble gas.

> Neon, like the other noble gasses, is non-reactive. It forms no known compounds.

ANALYSIS

After William Ramsey discovered neon in 1898, engineers and inventors tried in vain to find a practical use for the gas. Then in 1902, the French chemist/engineer Georges Claude (1870–1960) enclosed some neon in a glass tube and applied an electrical current to it. Claude was dazzled by neon's bright orange-red glow that we are so familiar with today. He produced several of his neon light bulbs and put them on public display in Paris in 1910. The public was fascinated by the colorful lights, but no one wanted to use them for home lighting.

Fortunately, Claude was not an inventor who gave up easily. He continued to work on his bulbs and found that he could shape them into long, thin tubes that could be made into letters and other shapes. After years of development, he formed a company in France called Claude Neon in 1923 to make and sell neon signs.

Claude sold his first two signs to a Los Angeles car dealer for $24,000. The signs spelled out "Packard" in brilliant orange letters. Neon quickly became a very popular advertising fixture in the United States and around the world. People marveled at the signs, and the reddish orange glow became known as "liquid fire." Later, other sign colors were created using argon gas, and then mercury and phosphorus vapors.

PERSISTENCE PAYS OFF

Georges Claude's determination serves as an inspiration to us today in our professional lives as well as personal goals. Despite early discouragements, he continued to research and develop his new technology. After 20 years of research, development, and product innovation, Claude was able to market his invention around the world. His signs enabled travelers to find their destinations and have lighted establishments from bars to churches for decades. By the time of his death at age 90, Georges Claude's invention had truly changed the world and brightened our lives.

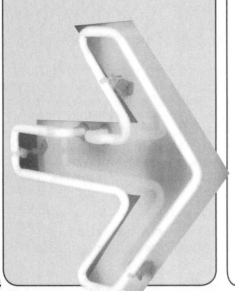

REACTION: *POWER SUPPLY*

Not even the fanciest, most expensive neon sign is very impressive when it is unplugged. But plug it in . . . connect it to its power supply . . . and it can attract a multitude or help travelers find their way in the darkness.

A Christian is a lot like a neon sign. The Bible tells us to let our "light so shine before men" and to glorify the Father in heaven (Matt. 5:16). But, like a sign, we can't shine unless we are "plugged in" to our power source.

Where does our "power" come from?

In the Great Commission, Jesus promised His disciples they would have spiritual power from heaven in order to spread the gospel. "But you shall receive power when the Holy Spirit has come upon you, and you shall be witnesses to Me in Jerusalem, and in all Judea and Samaria, and to the end of the earth" (Acts 1:8). Paul tells us that the promise of the same spiritual power extends to all believers. "For God has not given us a spirit of fear, but of power and of love and of a sound mind" (2 Tim. 1:7).

QUICK QUIZ

1. When exposed to an electric current, neon emits a _____ -colored light.

   a. white   b. reddish orange   c. purple   d. green

2. Neon is a (an) _____ _____.

   a. noble gas   b. diatomic molecule   c. corrosive gas   d. explosive compound

3. Neon comes from the Greek word *neos,* which means_____. (Fill in the blank.)

4. According to Matthew 5:15, how can we glorify our Heavenly Father?

5. Who discovered neon?

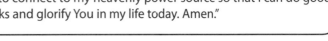

RESPONSE

"Heavenly Father, I realize that without You I am powerless. Help me to connect to my heavenly power source so that I can do good works and glorify You in my life today. Amen."

11
Na
22.9897

SODIUM: "The Salt of the Earth"

"You are the salt of the earth; but if the salt loses its flavor, how shall it be seasoned? It is then good for nothing but to be thrown out and trampled underfoot by men" (Matt. 5:13).

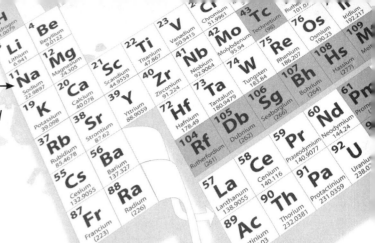

DATA

> Sodium was discovered by the prolific and brilliant Sir Humphry Davy in 1807.

> Davy called the element sodium because he derived it from caustic soda. However, the Germans and some other countries preferred the name natrium, from which the chemical symbol, Na, is derived.

> Sodium is a silvery metal whose surface oxidizes quickly when exposed to air. It is soft enough to be cut with a knife, and it melts in boiling water. (Melting point: 97.81°C)

> Sodium is most commonly found in combination with chlorine in the form of common salt (NaCl).

ANALYSIS

In the modern world, salt (sodium chloride or NaCl) is an inexpensive commodity. It is so cheap that it is spread on streets and sidewalks in cold climates to melt ice. Its most familiar use is to add flavor to foods, and many people consume too much salt for their own good. But in Jesus' day, this was not the case.

Salt was costly yet vitally important in everyday life, and the people had many uses for it. When Jesus called His followers "the salt of the earth," He implied that they had an important purpose in the world. The properties of salt reveal the powerful impact that Christians can have on society:

SALT IS A PRESERVATIVE. In Bible times, salt was rubbed into animal carcasses to retard the growth of bacteria that would otherwise cause the meat to go bad. This allowed for meat to be safely stored for long periods of time. Similarly, the presence of active Christian believers can positively impact a community by counteracting evil influences. Just as in the time of Sodom and Gomorrah, when God was willing to spare these sinful cities for the sake of ten righteous men (Gen. 18:32), Christians provide a preserving influence in the world.

SALT IS AN ANTISEPTIC. Newborn babies were bathed in saltwater and rubbed down with salt to protect their skin from infection (Ezek. 16:4). Saltwater is known to promote healing of wounds, and gargling with it can heal a sore throat. As Christians, we are to take the gospel to a world in need of its healing power.

SALT IS NEEDED FOR EXERTION. As any athlete knows, to function efficiently, the human body needs the proper balance of salt and other electrolytes, which are depleted during exertion. Roman soldiers were given salt rations to make sure they did not weaken in battle or on long marches.

SALT CAUSES THIRST. By setting a righteous example in a lost and dying world, Christians can cause unbelievers to hunger and thirst for the living water that only Christ can provide (Matt. 5:6).

SALT ADDS FLAVOR. In addition to the nutritional and preservative benefits of salt, sometimes it just makes our food taste better (Job 6:6–7). Christians who live by Bible principles should make the world more pleasant and a better place to live.

REACTION: *WITNESS*

When Jesus called for His followers to be the "salt of the earth," just what did He mean? Look at it like this.

Imagine that you go into a restaurant and order your favorite meal. But when you ask for some salt, you are told, "We're sorry, but we keep all of our salt locked up in a storage room." This is what our world is like when we only practice our Christianity inside of a church building. The Church is meant to be a blessing to the whole world, but to do so we must be the Church all the time and everywhere — not just behind closed doors on Sunday morning.

Jesus does not call for us to be the "salt of the church" or even the "salt of our homes." Instead He calls us to go out and be "witnesses" of Him "to the uttermost part of the earth" (Acts 1:8; KJV).

QUICK QUIZ

1. What is the chemical formula for table salt?

    a. $NaCl$ b. H_2O c. H_3BO_3 d. CO_2

2. In Bible times, salt was used for all of the following except _____.

    a. preservation of meat   b. protection from infection   c. flavoring foods   d. making potato chips

3. Sodium metal is _____.

    a. light and non-reactive   b. light and highly reactive   c. heavy and non-reactive   d. heavy and highly reactive

4. In Matthew 5:13, Jesus said that His followers were "the _____ of the _____." (Fill in the blanks.)

5. Sodium was discovered in 1807 by Sir _____ _____.

    a. Walter Scott   b. Paul McCartney   c. Lancelot   d. Humphry Davy

SODIUM CHLORIDE (TABLE SALT)

RESPONSE

The Bible uses an interesting phrase to describe the effect that the early Church had in the community. Christians were called people who "turned the world upside down" (Acts 17:6)! Like these early believers, sometimes we have to turn our own lives upside-down (like a saltshaker pouring out its salt) in order to be the witnesses that Jesus called us to be.

"Lord, how can I be the salt of the earth today? How can I improve the world around me and share the gospel as You wish? Help me to be vigilant for every opportunity. Thank You, Father."

MAGNESIUM: "The Blessings of Humility"

"So he [Naaman] went down and dipped seven times in the Jordan, according to the saying of the man of God [Elisha]; and his flesh was restored like the flesh of a little child, and he was clean. And he returned to the man of God, he and all of his aides, and came and stood before him; and he said, "Indeed, now I know there is no God in all the earth, except in Israel . . . " (2 Kings 5:14–15).

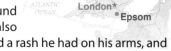

DATA

> The prolific and brilliant chemist Sir Humphry Davy discovered magnesium in 1808.

> Davy named it after one of the minerals that he found it in: magnesia, which in turn was named for the region of Greece (Magnesia) where it was discovered.

> Magnesium is a soft, silvery-white metal similar to lithium but more reactive.

> Magnesium forms several salts that are known to have healthful properties.

> Magnesium is one of the "alkaline earth" metals that make up the second column of the periodic table.

Sir Humphry Davy

ANALYSIS

In 1618 Henry Wicker, a farmer near the town of Epsom, England, was looking for a new place to water his livestock due to a drought. His cattle refused to drink from one particular spring, and he soon found out why. The water had a bitter taste. But Wicker also found that the water had healthful effects: it healed a rash he had on his arms, and it acted as a laxative.

As word of Wicker's discovery spread, people came from all over to sample the water from this spring. Epsom became the first "spa town" in England. Many inns and other businesses sprang up there. Europe already had several spas, but Epsom soon attracted visitors from the continent who bathed in the spas and bought barrels of its water to take with them. (Reliable, safe laxatives were hard to find in those days.)

Later, a doctor named Nehemiah Drew found that evaporating water from the springs of Epsom left behind a powdery, salty residue. In 1695 Drew received a patent for this new product, which he called "Epsom salts." (Even today you can still find Epsom salts in any drugstore and many doctors prescribe it.) Yet, for over a century, no one knew exactly what the substance was that made Epsom's water so remarkable.

In the early 1800s Sir Humphry Davy had already discovered several elements by subjecting minerals to electrolysis. In 1808 he tested two more minerals: the legendary Epsom salts and magnesia, a mineral named for the Greek region where it was first found. Davy found a common ingredient in both: a soft, silvery metal. He called this new element magnesium. He later identified Epsom salts as the compound magnesium sulfate ($MgSO_4$). He also identified magnesia as magnesium oxide (MgO), the main ingredient in another healthful product: Milk of Magnesia.

REACTION: *AND HIS FLESH WAS RESTORED*

Henry Wicker found healing in an undesirable water source. The Bible tells a similar story about a man called Naaman. Although he was a mighty general of the Syrian army, Naaman had a problem. He had leprosy. He tried every cure in his country before journeying to Israel to see the prophet Elisha.

The prophet told him to bathe in the Jordan River to be cured. At first Naaman refused. He thought it was beneath him to wash in a muddy Jewish river. But then he listened to some wise counsel (one of his own servants!), and he humbled himself. When he followed Elisha's command, Naaman was cured. (You can read the whole story in 2 Kings, chapter 5.)

A surprising comparison of these stories and the blessings that followed humility appears below:

	HENRY WICKER	NAAMAN
1. Hardship	Drought — no water for cattle	Stricken with leprosy
2. Hunt for solution	Traveled to Epsom	Traveled to Israel
3. Humble action required	Drink water rejected even by cattle	Listened to servant, washed in a foreign river
4. Healthy result	Skin treatment and laxative	Healing of leprosy
5. Help for others	Health spa and Epsom salts	Word of God spread to Syria

QUICK QUIZ

1. What English chemist discovered magnesium?

2. A healthful form of magnesium, called _____ salts, was named after the town where it was first found in England.

   a. London   b. Portsmouth   c. Liverpool   d. Epsom

3. Henry Wicker discovered a spring with bitter-tasting water that had a (an) _____ effect on the digestive system. (Fill in the blank.)

4. As a result of Henry Wicker's discovery, his hometown became a famous _____ town. (Fill in the blank.)

5. In the Book of 2 Kings, Naaman was required to bathe how many times in the Jordan River to be cleansed of leprosy?

"Out of the same mouth proceed blessings and cursing. My brethren, these things ought not to be so. Does a spring send forth fresh water and bitter from the same opening?"

—James 3:10-11

RESPONSE

"By humility and the fear of the LORD are riches and honor and life" (Prov. 22:4).

"Lord, I pray that I will never be too proud to receive the blessings that You intend for me. Even when they come from unexpected places. Amen."

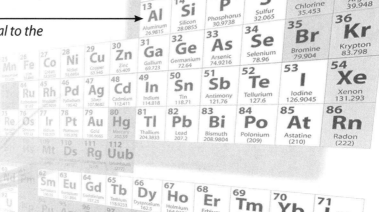

ALUMINUM: "Laus Deo"

"And these stones shall be for a memorial to the children of Israel forever" (Josh. 4:7).

DATA

> Aluminum is the third most abundant element (8 percent) in the earth's crust, after oxygen (47 percent) and silicon (28 percent). It is mostly found as alumina (Al_2O_3).

> Sir Humphry Davy proposed the name "alumium" (from the chemical alum) for the element in 1807, 20 years before it was isolated. Later the name was changed to aluminum.

> In 1825 the Danish chemist Hans Christian Oersted produced an impure sample of aluminum, and some credit him for aluminum's discovery.

> But in 1827 the German chemist Fredrick Wohler made the first high purity aluminum, and some consider Wohler to be the discoverer.

> A student of Wohler, William Frishmuth (1830–1893), moved from Germany to Philadelphia in 1855, where he continued to work in metallurgy. Frishmuth received 12 U.S. patents, including 3 for extracting aluminum.

> In Europe the metal is called aluminium — pronounced al-yoo-min-ee-um.

ANALYSIS

Today, aluminum is abundant and inexpensive. Aluminum soft drink cans, pie pans, and even gum wrappers are all considered disposable. But in the late 1800s, this was not the case. Aluminum was a "new" metal that most people had never heard of. Only a few people in the whole world could prepare it. Due to its scarcity, its price was about the same as silver. Aluminum was then a rare and unique metal, and it was about to be chosen for a special honor.

The foundation for the Washington Monument had been laid in 1848. However, due to financial and social problems (including the Civil War!), construction of the monument was halted several times. The structure would not be completed until 1885. As it was nearing completion, there was one final design decision to be made: how would the finished monument be protected from lightning?

Lightning rods had been in use ever since Benjamin Franklin designed the first one in 1749. But the Washington Monument was the tallest structure in the world at that time, and no one was quite sure how to make a lightning rod for it or even what to make it out of. Iron or steel could have been used, but either of these would rust away, leaving a brown stain. Copper or brass would last longer but would leave ugly greenish streaks down the side of the monument.

Fortunately, during the long construction period of the monument, aluminum became available. William Frishmuth, a student of the German chemist who first purified aluminum, had moved to Philadelphia in 1855, where he started a foundry (which eventually would become the Alcoa Aluminum Company). In 1885, Frishmuth was hired to cast "a perfect piece of workmanship" — an aluminum pyramid to form the cap of the Washington Monument. Aluminum's high electrical conductivity, durability, and non-staining character made it the perfect metal to protect the monument from lightning.

Frishmuth had a lot of fun with the pyramid. The country was quite excited about the monument's completion, and after taking about two months to make the pyramid (which is about nine inches tall and six inches wide at the base), Frishmuth delayed its delivery to Washington and took it to New York City, where he charged people a small fee to "step over the top of the Washington Monument."

REACTION: *A MONUMENT TO A GODLY MAN*

In the 19th Century, the American people knew that the Washington Monument was a special structure. Even today it is the tallest freestanding stone structure in the world, and then it was the tallest building of any kind.

But more importantly, the monument was built to honor a truly godly man, the father of the country, whose public speeches and writings were filled with references to God and His providence. In his first inaugural address, George Washington stated:

> *"No people can be bound to acknowledge and adore the Invisible Hand which conducts the affairs of men more than the people of the United States."* [1]

In the first Thanksgiving proclamation Washington stated:

> *"It is the duty of all nations to acknowledge the providence of Almighty God, to obey his will, to be grateful for his benefit, and humbly to implore his protection and favor."* [2]

So it is only appropriate that Washington's monument should be filled from bottom to top with references to God. And so it is. From the cornerstone, which contains a Bible, to memorial plaques with biblical inscriptions donated by churches and civic groups from across the country and around the world and placed in many of the stairway landings . . . praises to God and Bible verses can be found throughout the monument.

Finally, the east side of the aluminum pyramid, the side facing the rising sun, contains the elegantly simple, two-word Latin inscription: *Laus Deo.* In English this means "Praise God." How fitting that this godly man would be honored in this way. And that aluminum, the newly discovered metal with ideal physical properties, would be the medium to convey that message to future generations of Americans.

---

1 First inaugural, April 30, 1789
2 October 3, 1789

QUICK QUIZ

1. Aluminum is the _____ abundant element in the earth's crust.

   a. most   b. second most   c. third most   d. least

2. William Frishmuth, who made the pyramid-shaped cap for the Washington Monument, was a student of the German chemist who produced aluminum. What was his teacher's name?

3. The main purpose of the aluminum cap on the Washington Monument was for protection of the monument from lightning. Aluminum was the perfect metal to use for this purpose because of which of its properties?

   a. It conducts electricity   b. It is non-staining   c. It does not corrode   d. All of the above

4. What historic event interrupted the construction of the Washington Monument?

5. The Latin phrase "Laus Deo," which is engraved on the cap of the Washington Monument, means _____ _____ in English. (Fill in the blanks.)

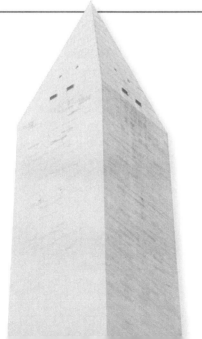

RESPONSE

The Washington Monument is 555 feet tall. Why was it built to this height? Is 555 some sort of magic number? Actually, the highest land elevation within the District of Columbia is 555 feet above sea level. Since the monument's base is a little above sea level, the top of the monument was certain to be the highest point in the District.

As a result, when the sun rises over the eastern horizon, the first thing that its light shines on each day is the brilliant aluminum cap of the Washington Monument and the words of praise: *Laus Deo.*

"Heavenly Father, help me to praise You each morning and to put Your glory as the highest priority in my life. Thank You for the Christian heritage I have received. Amen."

> *The memory of the just is blessed* (Prov. 10:7; KJV).

(From a memorial stone placed at the 260 foot landing of the Washington Monument.)

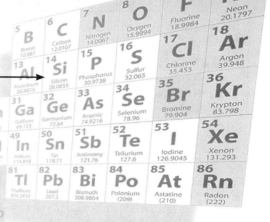

SILICON: "As the sand… on the seashore"

"Blessing I will bless you, and multiplying I will multiply your descendants as the stars of the heaven and as the sand which is on the seashore; and your descendants shall possess the gates of their enemies" (God, to Abraham; Gen. 22:17).

DATA

> Silicon is a dark-colored crystalline element in its pure form, but it is most familiar to us as the compound silica (silicon dioxide or SiO_2), which makes up most types of sand.

> The name silicon is from the Latin word *silex*, meaning "flint."

> In 1824 Swedish chemist Jons Berzulius produced high-quality samples of silicon, and he is credited with its discovery (although other scientists may have produced impure silicon earlier).

> Silicon in the second most common element in the earth's crust (after oxygen).

> Silicon dioxide in rocks, minerals, and sand is the most common chemical compound on earth (besides water).

ANALYSIS

One of the most important promises in the Bible was God's covenant with Abraham in Genesis 22. He said Abraham would be the father of a great nation. As a symbol of His promise, God used a substance that Abraham knew very well: sand. Just imagine standing on the seashore with your feet in the sand and bending down to count each tiny grain. Of course, that's impossible. Yet when Abraham was an old man with only one heir, God promised him that his offspring would be like the sand on the seashore.

AND GOD KEPT HIS PROMISE IN TWO WAYS.

First, in numbers. Abraham was the father of Israel. Through Abraham's son Isaac and grandson Jacob, a mighty nation prospered in the Middle East. Later, when they were held captive in Egypt, a great leader named Moses led Abraham's descendents out of slavery and into the Promised Land. The nation prospered under Saul, then the house of David, before hard times came again. Through it all, the people of Israel have persevered and revered the name of God and their ancient father Abraham. The Jewish people have spread around the world and have excelled in many fields, from science and literature to business and entertainment. Truly, Abraham's people became as innumerable as the grains of sand.

There is a second way that God kept His promise to Abraham that goes unnoticed. Arenologists, scientists who study and collect sand, categorize it by color. Some shores are covered with dazzling white sand made of weathered quartz (SiO_2) with virtually no pigments. Equally beautiful, beaches of volcanic islands like Tahiti feature striking black sand from eroded igneous rock. And of course, sand exists in every shade in between, from beige to yellow to brown, depending on the pigments in the grains.

Beaches come in as many shades as the people who enjoy them. And so do Abraham's children.

REACTION: ABRAHAM: "THE FATHER OF US ALL"

The New Testament tells us that Abraham's children are not only the Jews, but also all of us who have accepted Jesus Christ as our brother and Savior. Paul said that the promises made to Abraham's descendents apply to his children under the law (the Jews) and his children by faith (Christians), because "Abraham . . . is the father of us all" (Rom. 4:16). In Galatians 3:16, Paul again explains that we are all Abraham's descendants through Christ. Abraham is mentioned 72 times in the New Testament: of all the Old Testament figures, only Moses is mentioned more often.

Just as Abraham was probably amazed to think his descendents would be as innumerable as sand grains, surely he could not have imagined that people across the world, from pale Norwegians to dark-skinned Africans, and every shade in between . . . as many hues as the sands of the oceans . . . would come to accept one of his distant grandchildren, Jesus of Nazareth, as their Lord and Savior.

QUICK QUIZ

1. Most of the world's sand is made of silicon dioxide or SiO_2, which is also called _____. (Fill in the blank.)

2. Silicon was discovered in 1824 by _____ _____. (Fill in the blanks.)

3. In Galatians 3:16, _____ tells us that Christians are all the spiritual children of Abraham. (Fill in the blank.)

4. God promised Abraham that his children would be like the "sand on the seashore." Christians are like sand in which of the following ways?

   a. All sand is the same color   b. Sand grains are numerous and always white   c. Sand comes in every shade from white to black   d. Sand is soft

5. Scientists who study sand are known as _____. (Fill in the blank.)

RESPONSE

"Pardon me, but your epidermis is showing, sir.

I couldn't help but note your shade of melanin.

I tip my hat to the wisdom of your Maker, 'cause I

See the beauty in the tones of our skin.

"Colored People," DC Talk, 1985.

"Heavenly Father, help me to have faith like Abraham, to hold fast to Your promises and to believe Your every word. Help me to never forget that all of us are Your children."

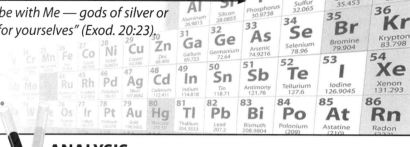

15	
P	
30.9738	

PHOSPHORUS: "All That Glitters Is Not Gold"

"You shall not make anything to be with Me — gods of silver or gods of gold you shall not make for yourselves" (Exod. 20:23).

DATA

> Phosphorus was discovered in 1669 by Hennig Brand (sometimes spelled Brandt).

> Elemental phosphorus exists in three forms: white phosphorus (a waxy solid), red phosphorus (a bright red powder), and black phosphorus (a reddish black crystal).

> Its name comes from the Greek word *phosphoros,* meaning "light bearing" or "luminous."

> Phosphorus is considered to be the 14th element discovered by man.

> Dietary phosphorus is essential for all forms of life; human urine contains around 20 to 40 parts per million of phosphorus.

> Today phosphorus is produced from minerals, and most of it goes into the manufacture of fertilizer.

ANALYSIS

There is a saying that goes all the way back to Aristotle: "All that glitters is not gold." This proverb especially applies to the early history of phosphorus. Stories of discovery of the elements can be tales of inspiration, brilliance, or just plain luck. But the story of phosphorus is certainly the most disgusting of all! And the man who found it was probably the most eccentric of all the discoverers of elements.

Hennig Brand was born in the 1620s in Hamburg, Germany. As a young man, he left home to become a soldier. When he returned home, he called himself "Dr. Brand," though there is no record of his getting any degree. Then he married a wealthy widow and used her money to build a laboratory where he intended to create gold!

In Brand's time, long before our modern understanding of atoms and elements, there was a common belief that gold could be made from other substances. This was the basis of the ancient practice called alchemy. Alchemists believed that gold was the purest substance and that other metals, like lead, iron, or even rocks and dirt, could be turned into gold by purifying them . . . if one could just find the right formula. Some alchemists were like scientists, motivated by a thirst for knowledge, but as you can imagine, most saw alchemy as a way to amass great riches. Hennig Brand was apparently one of the latter.

Somehow Brand got the idea that the yellow color of urine meant that it contained gold. So he went to the German army and got permission to collect urine from all the soldiers at a certain camp. He especially wanted the urine of beer-drinkers, because beer has a yellow hue as well. After years of experiments, he produced not gold, but a mysterious substance that no one had ever seen before. Here is a brief version of his recipe: 1) Collect fifty buckets of urine. 2) Let it sit in the sun for two weeks until maggots begin to grow in it. 3) Boil the liquid (maggots and all). 4) Keep it in a cellar until it turns black. 5) Distill the black residue to produce a white, waxy paste. Brand didn't know it, but that paste was a new element: phosphorus. Brand's name for it was "cold fire" or "liquid gold."

Brand kept his discovery secret for six years. He learned he could store his "cold fire" under water for a long time, but when exposed to the air it would glow in the dark. He used its light to read at night. Sometimes it would even burst into flame. He found a way to make it into a spooky, glow-in-the-dark ink. But he could never turn his discovery into gold. Brand had spent much of his wife's fortune, so from time to time he would sell his phosphorus to other alchemists and eventually he was so desperate that he sold his secret. Soon others were making phosphorus and even taking credit for its discovery.

No one knows when Brand died, but it was probably after 1710. His last days were not in poverty but obscurity. Fortunately for history, an acquaintance later wrote down the true story of Brand's discovery; otherwise, the pretenders would have likely been given the credit.

Brand's discovery was remarkable even though he never found what he was looking for. He could have learned a lesson from Aristotle: All that glitters is not gold. Sometimes it's just urine.

REACTION: *FOOLS GOLD*

"Because you say, 'I am rich, have become wealthy, and have need of nothing' — and do not know that you are wretched, miserable, poor, blind, and naked — I counsel you to buy from Me gold refined in the fire, that you may be rich . . . " (Rev. 3:17–18).

Hennig Brand's phosphorus is not the only substance that has been confused with gold.

The mineral pyrite (FeS_2) is a shiny, yellow, metallic-looking compound that was often mistaken for gold in the old West. Another name for pyrite is "fool's gold." Some alloys of copper also look very similar to gold, and these have been fraudulently used as gold substitutes.

In Revelation 3:17 and 18, Jesus warns His followers against striving for fool's gold rather than spiritual wealth. He told the wealthy church of Laodicea that even though they thought they had "need of nothing," they were actually far from God and His standard of righteousness. In His eyes, they were "wretched, miserable, poor, blind, and naked." They were satisfied with the fool's gold of this world, but He had something better for them.

True gold, refined in the fire, will make us rich in a way that worldly riches never will.

QUICK QUIZ

1. Elemental phosphorus exists in three main forms, which include all of the following except for:

    a. a white, waxy solid   b. a red powder   c. a dark red crystal   d. a shiny metal

2. Phosphorus was first discovered in what bodily fluid?

    a. blood   b. saliva   c. urine   d. stomach acid

3. The main goal of alchemy was to create what substance?

4. The mineral iron pyrite is also called _____ _____. (Fill in the blanks.)

5. White phosphorus, when exposed to air, has what "spooky" property?

RESPONSE

"Heavenly Father, help me not to be fooled by the temptations and distractions of the world. Give me Your true gold, refined in the fire, that will make me truly rich. Amen."

16	
S	
32.065	

SULFUR: "Fire and Brimstone: God's Judgment"

"Then the LORD rained brimstone and fire on Sodom and Gomorrah, from the LORD out of the heavens" (Gen. 19:24).

DATA

> Sulfur was one of the nine elements known to the ancients (seven metals plus sulfur and carbon). It sometimes occurs in its pure form in nature.

> In 1777 French chemist Antoine Lavoisier showed that sulfur is an element.

> Sulfur is a yellow, brittle, nonmetal solid that burns easily.

> As an element, Sulfur is odorless and tasteless, but most of its compounds have strong taste and odor. Sulfur compounds are responsible for the odors of rotten eggs and beans.

> References to "brimstone" in the Bible usually refer to sulfur.

> Sulfur is important in the human diet in the form of protein and other nutrients.

ANALYSIS

The word brimstone comes from the Old English word *brynstan* meaning "burning stone." That is a good description of the element sulfur. Pieces of this hard, yellow solid burn easily when exposed to a flame. The gasses and smoke produced by burning sulfur are poisonous and can cause choking, loss of consciousness, or even death, depending on the level of exposure. Sulfur smoke has been used as a fumigant to rid buildings of vermin since the ancient Greeks. The biblical writers and even Christ himself used "fire and brimstone" as a perfect illustration of hell and God's judgment on the wicked.

"[O]n the day that Lot went out of Sodom, it rained fire and brimstone from heaven and destroyed them all. Even so will it be in the day when the Son of Man is revealed" (Luke 17:29–30). This is how Jesus described God's judgment on Sodom and Gomorrah from Genesis 19.

In the Book of Deuteronomy, God warns the Israelites that if they turn away from Him to worship false gods, even Israel herself could end up as a land of "brimstone, salt, and burning" where no grass or crops would grow, as an example to all other nations (Deut. 29:23).

Other verses in the Old Testament that describe God's judgment of "fire and brimstone" on the wicked are found in Job 18:15; Psalm 11:6; Isaiah 30:33, 34:9; and Ezekiel 38:22.

Some references to brimstone in the Book of Revelation may be prophetic allusions to chemical warfare: "fire, smoke and brimstone. By these three plagues a third of mankind was killed . . ." (Rev. 9:17–18). Elsewhere in Revelation "fire and brimstone" create the perfect vision of hell where Satan and the wicked are condemned (Rev. 14:10, 19:20, and 20:10).

The last mention of brimstone in the Bible is similar to the first in Genesis. It is folly for sinners to think they can escape God's ultimate judgment.

"But the cowardly, unbelieving, abominable, murderers, sexually immoral, sorcerers, idolaters, and all liars shall have their part in the lake which burns with fire and brimstone, which is the second death" (Rev. 21:8; NKJV).

REACTION: *CHRIST'S PATIENCE*

In Luke 9, Jesus wanted to stop in Samaria on His way to Jerusalem, so He sent His disciples, James and John, ahead to find a place to stay. In those days, inns were usually little more than brothels, so what the pair were really sent to do was to find someone willing to open up his home to Jesus and His band of followers. In this, the disciples had no luck. Now James and John were very hot-tempered individuals (Jesus even nicknamed them "sons of thunder" in Mark 3:17, due to their fiery dispositions), and they were very angry about being rejected by the Samaritans.

Inspired by Old Testament tales of God raining down fire and brimstone on evildoers (especially Elijah's story in 2 Kings 1), the "sons of thunder" suggested a similar fate for Samaria. "Lord, do You want us to command fire to come down from heaven and consume them, just as Elijah did?" (Luke 9:54).

But Jesus wanted to help His Samaritan neighbors, not condemn them. He could understand the Samaritans' reluctance to take in a radical rabbi from Israel and His band of rough disciples. Jesus always had a special place in His heart for these people that the Jews considered half-breed heretics (Luke 10:29–37; Acts 1:8; etc.).

Jesus rebuked James and John for their unforgiving spirits. "You do not know what manner of spirit you are of. For the Son of Man did not come to destroy men's lives but to save them" (Luke 9:55–56).

As followers of Jesus, we must not judge or condemn our fellow man. Like Jesus, we are to introduce them to salvation and the true faith of the Bible. Ultimately, God will judge them with His perfect wisdom and understanding. Like James and John, we should leave that judgment up to the Judge of the universe.

QUICK QUIZ

1. The biblical term for the substance we call sulfur is _____. (Fill in the blank.)

2. Many compounds of sulfur (such as hydrogen sulfide) have strong _____. (Fill in the blank.)

3. Which form of nutrient contains sulfur?

   a. carbohydrates   b. proteins   c. oils and fats   d. starches

4. In the Book of Revelation, the place of eternal punishment is described as a lake of _____ and _____.

5. In Luke 9, Jesus rebuked James and John for condemning what city?

   a. Samaria   b. Damascus   c. Bethlehem   d. Jerusalem

RESPONSE

Jesus told James and John, "You do not know what manner of spirit you are of." As close as they were to Christ, they still did not yet know the Holy Spirit and their relationship to Christ.

And what about us? What "manner of spirit" are we of? As baptized believers in Christ, we are of the Holy Spirit, whose fruits are "love, joy, peace, longsuffering, kindness, goodness, faithfulness, gentleness, self-control" (Gal. 5:22–23). Judgment and condemnation are not to be found on that list.

"Heavenly Father, perfect Judge of the world, thank You for sending Your Son Jesus to earth to deliver me from the fire and brimstone of hell and to lead me to You. Thank You for Your patience in dealing with me. Thank You for Your Word that shows me the love and patience of my Savior. Help me to always remember 'what manner of Spirit I am of.' Amen."

17

Cl

35.453

CHLORINE: "The Miracle Element"

"Though your sins are like scarlet, they shall be as white as snow"
(Isa. 1:18). "Wash me, and I shall be whiter than snow" (Ps. 51:7).

DATA

> Chlorine is a greenish yellow hazardous gas. It forms a diatomic molecule (Cl_2).

> Chlorine is a member of the halogen family, of the periodic table.

> Like all halogens, chlorine is very reactive. It is used to make many plastics, solvents, pesticides, etc.

> As the chloride ion (Cl^-), chorine is indispensable to all plant, animal, and human life.

> Chorine was discovered by the German Carl Wilhelm Scheele in 1774, and shown to be an element by Humphry Davy in 1810.

> Chlorine comes from the Greek *chloros* meaning "green."

> Some of the major uses of chlorine are as bleach and as a disinfectant.

> Chlorine added to drinking water kills typhoid fever, dysentery, cholera, Legionnaires' disease, and other disease germs.

ANALYSIS

In the 19th century a disease known as typhoid fever was a terrible scourge, especially in growing cities where many people lived in close proximity. Typhoid is spread through contaminated food or drinking water. It causes severe sickness throughout the body, especially the digestive system, including intestinal pain and bleeding. This bacterial disease killed thousands of people and sickened many more every year. The mortality rate from typhoid was about 30 percent. Of the 70 percent who survived, about 1 out of 20 would become "carriers" of the disease. The so-called "Typhoid Mary" of New York City was the most famous of these carriers (the first one identified in the United States), but many others unknowingly carried the bacteria in their bodies, spreading it by casual contact. The ability of typhoid fever to be carried by otherwise healthy survivors made it very difficult to control.

CHICAGO — EARLY 20TH CENTURY

By 1900 typhoid fever was a severe problem in Chicago, which had grown from a small town to a city of over two million people in about 80 years. In part, the story of Chicago's growth was a story of how the city met its needs for water supply and sewage disposal. Waste from stockyards and other industries added to its sewage. Parts of Chicago had been built on a swamp, and drainage was always a problem.

Originally, Chicagoans relied on septic tanks, but as the population grew, groundwater wells became contaminated, so sewers were constructed to take waste away from homes and into Lake Michigan. As growth continued, water wells were insufficient and the city resorted to drawing water from Lake Michigan itself. But by this time, a great amount of raw sewage was being dumped into the lake, so the city's engineers designed tunnels that went far out from shore in order to avoid human contamination. In 1867 a tunnel was built under the lake that went out for two and a half miles. However, they found that not even this remarkable engineering feat was enough to avoid the typhoid bacteria: longer tunnels were built, including a four-mile project in 1891. But wastes from the growing numbers of ships on Lake Michigan were an unavoidable source of contamination that continued to confound city officials.

CHLORINE TO THE RESCUE

Scattered outbreaks and full-scale epidemics continued; for example, 1,997 Chicagoans died from a typhoid outbreak in 1891. The city was desperate for a solution. As it turned out, it was a chlorine solution.

In the late 1800s the English had experimented with adding chlorine to drinking water, and in the early 1900s they began using it continuously. Based on the British results, Chicago started adding chlorine to their 800 million gallon per day drinking water supply.

The results were remarkable. Prior to chlorination, the typhoid death rate in Chicago was as high as 174 per 100,000 population. However, by 1916 the city's entire water supply had been chlorinated. The next year, there were only 456 typhoid cases, and all of these infections had come from drinking water from outside of Chicago or from contaminated milk or food.

Based on its effectiveness in Chicago, the use of chlorine soon spread across the United States. The national death rate dropped to practically zero by 1950 as over 98 percent of all water supplies in the United States added chlorine to their drinking water.

REACTION: *ROBES WASHED WHITE*

These are the ones who come out of the great tribulation, and washed their robes and made them white in the blood of the Lamb (Rev. 7:14).

Chlorine (Cl_2) is a powerful killer of bacteria. A relatively tiny amount of chlorine gas dissolved in a large water supply system makes it safe to drink. Also a small concentration of chlorine in wastewater keeps diseases from spreading downstream.

Campers often add a capful of chlorine bleach (NaOCl) to streamwater to kill any harmful bacteria before they drink it.

Chlorine is an excellent metaphor for the cleansing power of Christ's blood. The action of adding a little chlorine bleach to your laundry can make the whole load spotless and clean, and this reminds us of the saving power of Christ's blood. The blood that Jesus shed on the Cross is powerful enough to cleanse away the sins of everyone who has ever lived, if they would only believe in Him.

QUICK QUIZ

1. Chlorine is a member of the _____ family of elements. (Fill in the blank.)

2. Chlorine is added to drinking water to kill bacteria. Which waterborne disease was rampant in early 20th century Chicago?

   a. influenza   b. Legionnaires' disease   c. whooping cough   d. typhoid fever

3. A woman called "Typhoid Mary" spread disease in what U.S. city?

4. Chicago's water supply comes from which Great Lake?

5. Which of the following does *not* describe molecular chlorine?

   a. diatomic molecule   b. disinfectant   c. safe to inhale its vapors   d. greenish yellow gas

RESPONSE

"Father God, thank You for Your Son and His sacrifice. Christ's blood, shed on a dirty and vile cross, has flowed down through the ages to reach me just as I am. Thank You for washing away my sins and making me clean through Jesus. Amen."

18

Ar

39.948

ARGON: "The Lazy Gas"

"Go to the ant, you sluggard! Consider her ways and be wise" (Prov. 6:6).

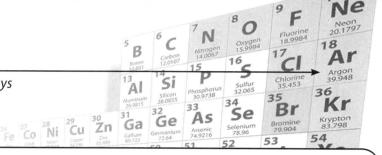

ANALYSIS

This is a story about a gas whose name means "lazy."

Nitrogen was discovered in 1772, and oxygen in 1774. Many experiments were done to quantify the amount of these two gasses in the atmosphere and for most of the 1800s, it was believed that air contained 21 percent oxygen and 79 percent nitrogen, and that was it (except for small amounts of water vapor, carbon dioxide, and dust). For over 100 years no one suspected that the air we breathe was any more complicated.

That understanding of the atmosphere's make-up made sense to the scientists of the day and helped to explain many things. For example, if you light a candle and place it inside a jar, the flame will burn approximately one-fifth of the air (the oxygen) in the jar before going out. There was still plenty of air left in the jar, but it was a type of air that would not burn. The non-burning air was assumed to be nitrogen.

In 1894 William Ramsey, a scientist who had experimented extensively with gasses, began a test of a quantity of air that had had all the oxygen removed from it: this was supposed to be pure nitrogen. He put the nitrogen in a reactor that contained magnesium and heated it up to a temperature so hot that it made even nitrogen (which is normally inert) react to form magnesium nitrite. But no matter how much he heated it, there was always a little bit of gas left, about 1/80th of the original volume. Ramsey concluded that this small remainder of gas was a new element. Since it was so unreactive, he called it "argon: the lazy one." (Ramsey would go on to discover or participate in the discovery of all of the other noble gasses: helium, neon, krypton, xenon, and radon.)

ARGON: LAZY BUT USEFUL

In the years since its discovery, argon has actually turned out to be quite useful, because of its inertness. And it is fairly inexpensive. Nowadays, argon can easily be gotten from the atmosphere by the fractional distillation of liquid air.

1. LIGHTBULBS. When you buy a regular screw-in light bulb, what you actually have is a glass container full of argon. From their invention in 1879, lightbulbs consisted of a metal filament (a thin wire) inside a glass bulb. When electricity flows through the filament, it heats up and begins to glow. To keep the hot filament from burning up, all of the air is removed from the bulb. However, in 1914 light bulb manufacturers began adding argon to replace the vacuum. Filling the bulb with non-reactive argon makes lightbulbs last longer by creating a "cushion of gas" around the filament.

2. WELDING. During World War I, arc-welding became common. Arc-welding is the use of electricity to heat metals to their melting points to form joints between two pieces of metal. Unfortunately, when metals are welded in a normal atmosphere, oxygen in the air combines with the hot metals to form metal oxides, which are impurities that weaken the joints. In 1929 welders began using tanks of argon to blow continuous streams of inert gas on weld joints, keeping the oxygen away until the weld cooled.

3. OTHER USES. Argon has other uses in industry where it is important to eliminate oxygen and nitrogen. Titanium, an important high-strength metal which is very reactive to oxygen when heated, cannot be produced without it. Also, transistors and other computer parts are manufactured surrounded by argon.

DATA

> Argon is a noble gas. It is the third most common gas in the atmosphere (after nitrogen and oxygen), making up 0.93 percent of the air we breathe. There is about 30 times as much argon in the atmosphere as carbon dioxide. (Argon is the only noble gas that is not considered to be rare.)

> Argon was co-discovered in 1894 by the Englishmen Sir William Ramsey, a chemist, and Lord Rayleigh, a physicist. They received a $10,000 prize from the Smithsonian Institution. In 1904 they received the Nobel Prizes for chemistry and physics, respectively, for their discovery.

> The element's name is from the Greek prefix *a* meaning "without" and *ergos* meaning "work." Therefore, argon means inert or lazy.

REACTION: *LAZY FAITH*

God created argon to be the lazy gas of the periodic table. But we Christians ought not to be lazy. We should be like Jesus, who said, "I must be about My Father's business" (Luke 2:49).

Chapter 2 of the Book of James warns against having "faith without works." The original Greek phrase James used was *pistos argos*, which can be translated as "lazy faith."

"But do you want to know, O foolish man, that faith [*pistos*] without works [*argos*] is dead?" (James 2:20; *NKJV*).

As an example of "lazy faith," James gives the following: "If a brother or sister is naked and destitute of daily food, and one of you says to them, 'Depart in peace, be warmed and filled,' but you do not give them the things which are needed for the body, what does it profit?" (James 2:15–16).

In other words, according to James, having a lazy faith is like having no faith at all.

QUICK QUIZ

1. The Greek word *argos* means _____. (Fill in the blank)

2. Argon makes up almost _____ percent of our atmosphere.

   a. one   b. five   c. ten   d. fifty

3. The discoverer of argon and other noble gasses was _____ _____. (Fill in the blanks.)

4. Argon gas is used to fill_____.

   a. incandescent lightbulbs   b. hot air balloons   c. jet fuel tanks   d. ping pong balls

5. Argon is needed to produce what important high strength metal?

RESPONSE

"Lord, I want my faith to be alive and strong. I want the works of kindness and righteousness that I do to reflect the true faith in my heart so that no one will ever doubt that I am Your follower. Help me not to have a lazy faith. Help me, like Jesus, to always 'be about My Father's business.' Amen."

19	
K	
39.098	

POTASSIUM: "Potash: First American Industry"

"To console those who mourn in Zion, to give them beauty for ashes, the oil of joy for mourning, the garment of praise for the spirit of heaviness, that they may be called trees of righteousness, the planting of the LORD, that He may be glorified" (Isa. 61:3).

DATA

> Potassium, in its pure form, is a soft, waxy, silvery metal. It is so reactive that, when it makes contact with water, it bursts into flame, producing corrosive potassium hydroxide and explosive hydrogen gas, according to the equation: $2K + 2H_2O \rightarrow 2KOH + H_2$.

> In 1807 potassium was the first element discovered by Sir Humphry Davy.

> Davy named it potassium because he derived it from a chemical called "potash" (a crude form of potassium carbonate, $KHCO_3$).

> The symbol, K, is from the Latin word for potash, *kalium*.

ANALYSIS

This is a story about how something quite valuable was made from something we may consider to be worthless: ashes.

The most important industrial chemical of the 18th century was potash. It was vital to the manufacture of commodities including glass, soap, textiles, gunpowder, drugs, and dyes. England had a great demand for potash, and the main source of potash was the ashes of trees. Unfortunately, England had used much of its forests for fuel, so its potash had to be gotten from elsewhere. In pre-Revolutionary times, that source was America.

Potash was originally known as pot-ashes, because of the way it was made. Trees were burned in huge open fires and the ashes were gathered, mixed with water, and placed in large iron vats that were called "pots." The mixture was boiled down to produce a thick black residue. This residue was a crude but valuable form of potassium carbonate ($KHCO_3$).

The best potash came from hardwood trees like elm, maple, ash, and hickory. As potash demand grew, the vast numbers of settlers were drawn to the hardwood forests of New England and Southern Canada. (Southern forests were mostly softer woods that did not produce good potash.) The settlers generally used burning to clear out the impenetrable virgin forests. Potash generated from the resulting ashes could often bring a better income than farming, so when settlers had cleared an area of its hardwood, they were likely to burn down their wooden homes for more ashes (and to retrieve the valuable iron nails) and leave their homesteads behind for more forested land.

The importance of the potash trade in America, before and after the Revolution, has largely been forgotten. But in those days, nearly every northern town had an "ashery" where farmers could sell ashes. European surnames like Ash and Asher came from this profession. The first patents granted by the United States and by Canada were for improved ways of making potash. From the time of the Revolution until the 1860s, the United States was the world's largest producer of potash. Around that time, the Germans began mining underground deposits of high-quality potash. Mining potash was less expensive than making it from ashes, so the American potash industry declined rapidly. But its trade was an important factor in the early growth of New England. It also brought revenue to the United States at a crucial point in its development, including funding for the American Revolution.

In 1807 Humphry Davy discovered a previously unknown metal in potash, which he named potassium, as an indication of its source.

REACTION: *ASHES TO ASHES, DUST TO DUST*

"Earth to earth, ashes to ashes, dust to dust; in sure and certain hope of the Resurrection unto eternal life." This oft-quoted verse is not from the Bible. It is from the Anglican Church's *Book of Common Prayer*. It is often recited at funerals. Of course, the verse hearkens back to God's creation of Adam from the "dust of the ground" (Gen. 2:7 and 3:19).

Apparently, Abraham was keenly aware of his own "earthly" nature when he spoke (actually argued) with God himself to request leniency for Sodom in Genesis 18:27: "Then Abraham answered and said, 'Indeed now, I who am but dust and ashes have taken it upon myself to speak to the Lord.'" What better way to show humility before God than to acknowledge that you already know your ultimate fate!

Other saints of the Bible made similar expressions of humility when they found themselves face to face with the Almighty. For example, Job said, "Behold, I am vile; what shall I answer You?" and later he repented in "dust and ashes" (Job 40:4 and 42:6). Isaiah admitted he was "a man of unclean lips" (Isa. 6:5). Mary, in the presence of the archangel, simply said, "Behold the maidservant of the Lord" (Luke 1:38).

How amazing it is that God takes the most common elements of the earth, like carbon, hydrogen, oxygen, iron, calcium, and potassium, and places within such "dust and ashes" a human soul and a living spirit! Even more amazing is that when we turn to Him and accept Christ as Savior, His Holy Spirit comes to reside within these created bodies. No wonder the angels of heaven are astonished (1 Pet. 1:12).

QUICK QUIZ

1. The most important industrial chemical in the 18th century was called_____. (Fill in the blank.)

2. What type of trees were the best for producing the chemical described in question 1?

    a. fruit trees   b. palm trees   c. hardwood trees   d. pine trees

3. What method was used to clear most of the forestland in the northwest United States?

    a. clear cutting   b. burning   c. selective cutting   d. farming

4. According to Genesis 2:7, God made Adam from the "_____ of the _____." (Fill in the blanks.)

5. Who discovered potassium?

RESPONSE

"Heavenly Father, what a privilege it is that we come before You with our praises and petitions! Like Abraham, help us to ever be mindful of our humble state, yet as adopted children and brothers and sisters of Christ to come boldly before Your throne. Amen."

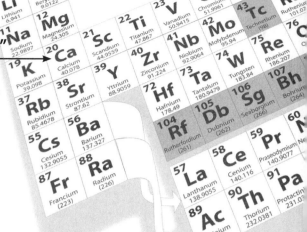

20
Ca
40.078

CALCIUM: "Fearfully and Wonderfully Made"

*"I will praise You, for I am fearfully and wonderfully made; marvelous are Your works, and that my soul knows very well. My **frame** [literally, "my **bones**" or "my skeleton"] was not hidden from You, when I was made in secret, and skillfully wrought in the lowest parts of the earth" (Ps. 139:14–15, emphasis added).*

DATA

> In 1808 calcium was the third element discovered by Sir Humphry Davy.

> Calcium is a hard, silvery white metal and is the fifth most common element in the earth's crust.

> The name calcium is from the Latin word *calx*, meaning "lime."

> Calcium is needed for bones and teeth, and for the proper operation of bodily systems, such as the muscles and the heart. Most people get their calcium requirement from dairy products.

ANALYSIS

Our bodies contain about 1.5 percent calcium. So if you weigh 200 pounds, about 3 pounds of your weight is calcium. About 99 percent of the calcium in your body is in your bones and teeth. How that calcium gets there is quite a story.

1. CALCIUM IN THE SOIL. Calcium is water-soluble, and there is quite a lot of it in most types of soil. If necessary, a farmer can enhance the amount of calcium in his land by spreading crushed limestone ($CaCO_3$) or gypsum ($CaSO_4$) on his fields after each harvest.

2. CALCIUM IN PLANT CELL WALLS. As plants grow, they combine carbon dioxide (CO_2) from the air and water (H_2O) from the soil to form long chains of a substance called cellulose. This cellulose forms the matrix or framework that surrounds and supports the individual cells of a plant. You might think of cellulose as the "skeleton" of the plant.

This cellulose skeleton is strong but not stiff. Some plants, such as grains and grass, need to grow tall and straight so their blades can absorb sunlight. These plants need another substance to cause this framework to stand up: calcium. Calcium ions in the soil (Ca^{++}) are absorbed through the plants' roots. These ions are embedded into the cellulose "skeleton," making the blades of grass strong enough to stand up in all weather conditions, so they can absorb sunlight.

3. CALCIUM IN MILK. Grasses and grains are the major component of a cow's diet. A pregnant cow needs an enormous amount of calcium for the bones of her unborn calf to grow properly. She must eat quite a lot of grass to supply that need. After birth, the rapidly growing calf must get its calcium requirements satisfied by its mother's milk. That's why milk is such a good source of calcium. A cow is practically a "calcium factory."

4. CALCIUM IN OUR BONES. Like grain and blades of grass, our bones also have a two-component structure. The strong yet flexible protein collagen forms the matrix in which the cells of our bones grow. But bones need calcium to stiffen and strengthen the collagen matrix to allow us to walk and work and lift heavy loads. Without enough calcium, bones become weak and breakable. Calcium is found in dark green, leafy vegetables, but the best source is milk and dairy products.

This is the amazing pathway that God designed to take calcium from a mineral in the soil to our bones and teeth. Truly David was right when he said, "Marvelous are Your works, and that my soul knows very well" (Ps. 139:14).

REACTION: *THE SPIRITUAL DIET*

As newborn babes, desire the sincere milk of the word, that you may grow thereby (1 Pet. 2:2).

Just as calves and infants need the calcium supplied by their mother's milk to grow strong and healthy, "newborn" Christians need the spiritual nutrition that comes from the Word of God.

THE NEW BIRTH

When a person becomes a Christian, the Bible says he or she is "born again." Jesus explained it like this: "Most assuredly, I say to you, unless one is born again, he cannot see the kingdom of God" (John 3:3). The new birth marks the beginning of the believer's entry into the body of Christ and his or her spiritual journey.

THE PURE MILK OF THE WORD

Peter speaks of the need for new Christians to draw nourishment from God's Word: "As newborn babes, desire the sincere milk of the word, that you may grow thereby" (1 Pet. 2:2; see also Heb. 5:12–14). The "milk of the word" refers to the basic doctrines of our faith: things that many of us may have learned in Sunday school. Just as in math or science, you have to learn the basics before you can take on the more complex lessons.

SOLID FOOD (THE MEAT OF DOCTRINE)

Newborn Christians are exciting to see. They bring joy to a church, just like babies bring joy to a family. But they are expected to grow up eventually. This was Paul's complaint to the carnal Christians in the Corinthian church. "I fed you with milk, and not with solid food; for until now you were not able to receive it, and even now you are still not able" (1 Cor. 3:2). Paul is basically telling these Christians to grow up, take the baby bottle out, and really dig into God's Word.

When they do that, they can say like Jeremiah: "Your words were found, and I ate them, and Your word was to me the joy and rejoicing of my heart" (Jer. 15:16).

QUICK QUIZ

1. Approximately _____ percent of the human body is made of calcium.
    a. 0.1   b. 1.5   c. 3   d. 5

2. Calcium is common in _____.
    a. soil   b. water   c. air   d. rain

3. TRUE or FALSE: Calcium helps to stiffen the stalks and leaves of grasses and grains.

4. Paul refers to the basic, simple doctrines of the Christian faith as "milk." He says as new believers mature in the faith, they should advance from spiritual milk to "_____." (Fill in the blank.)

5. What type of food is the best source of calcium in the human diet?

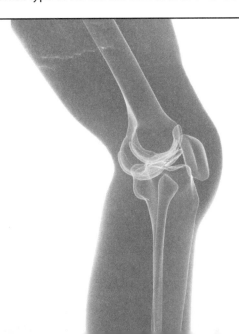

RESPONSE

The Bible is so simple that a child or a mentally handicapped person can have a full and deep understanding of it, yet the smartest person can dedicate his whole life to its study and never uncover all of the truth it contains.

"God of creation, thank You for Your Word. It is the true source of wisdom, justice, goodness, and the knowledge of salvation. Most of all, when we read it, asking for the Spirit to guide us, it points us to Jesus, who draws us closer to You. Help me to study it and go beyond the milk of the newborn. I want to dig into the meat so that I can grow to be the strong Christian You want me to be. Amen."

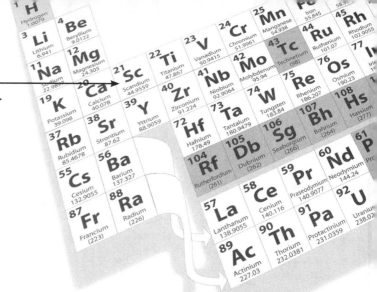

21
Sc
44.9559

SCANDIUM: "A Little Does A Lot"

"A little leaven leavens the whole lump" (Gal. 5:9).

DATA

> Scandium is a silvery-white, fairly soft metal.

> Scandium was discovered in 1879 by the Swedish chemist Lars Fredrik Nilson. He named the element in honor of Scandinavia, his homeland and the place where he discovered it.

> The existence of scandium was predicted by Mendeleyev in 1871.

> Scandium's applications in industry have been few due to its relative scarcity, but recent discoveries of ore deposits may increase its use.

ANALYSIS

Metallurgy is the study of metals and their properties. It includes extracting metals from their ores, purifying them, and creating useful alloys and objects. Even though metallurgy's beginnings are ancient (see Gen. 4:22), we are a long way from running out of new discoveries in this field. Due to the large number of metals and the fact that the properties of their alloys are not always predictable, metallurgy remains a vibrant and growing area of study.

Scandium has long been considered a scarce metal, and in the past it has been difficult to refine its ores. However, with the discovery of new deposits of scandium and the development of new techniques to refine it, the price of the metal is coming down and its availability is increasing. So scientists are now trying to find beneficial uses for scandium. One of the most promising is to use scandium as an alloy with aluminum in aeronautics.

Aluminum is strong, lightweight, and abundant. As such, it is nearly the ideal material for the bodies and wings of airplanes. However, aluminum has its shortcomings.

Aluminum does not rust like iron, but when pure aluminum is exposed to air it forms a thin outer layer of aluminum oxide, AlO_2 (which protects the remaining aluminum from further oxidation). This oxide layer is not as smooth as the pure metal, so it causes an aerodynamic drag effect. To avoid drag, planes must be painted. Paint adds about 1 to 2 percent to a plane's weight. The extra weight increases the amount of fuel needed for each flight.

Also, aluminum forms weak joints when welded, so planes made of aluminum are held together with metal rivets. This can add up to 10 percent to a plane's weight.

However, the addition of a small amount of scandium (often much less than one percent) miraculously changes the aluminum's properties. The resulting alloy is referred to as "scandium-reinforced aluminum" or Al-Sc. This alloy can be welded to produce very strong joints, which could eliminate the need for relatively heavy rivets. Also, Al-Sc does not corrode in the atmosphere, eliminating the need to paint the aircraft. While this small amount of scandium adds to the total cost of the aircraft, cost savings in these other areas should eventually more than offset this increased cost.

Within the next ten years, scandium-reinforced aluminum alloys have the potential to revolutionize the aerospace industry and bring about the next generation of aerospace technology.

REACTION: *A LITTLE LEAVEN*

And again He [Jesus] said, "To what shall I liken the kingdom of God? It is like leaven, which a woman took and hid in three measures of meal till it was all leavened " (Luke 13:20–21).

"For the bread of God is He who comes down from heaven and gives life to the world" (John 6:33).

It only takes a small amount of scandium to bring about radical changes in the properties of aluminum. In the same way, a little bit of leaven or yeast added to a large amount of dough causes major changes.

On several occasions in the Old Testament (Gen. 18:6, 19:3; Exod. 12:8), people had to leave their homes to avoid danger, and the bread they took with them was unleavened because it had to be made in a hurry. Unleavened bread is nutritious but dry and tasteless. God required the use of unleavened bread during Passover to remind the Jews of the difficulties of times past and of God's deliverance. Bread without leaven is even called the "bread of affliction," in light of its association with unpleasantness (Deut. 16:3).

In a parable, Jesus described the kingdom of God as being "like leaven." Many Bible scholars believe Jesus was referring to the ability of a small amount of yeast mixed in with dough to improve the bread's flavor and texture. Bread that is baked with leaven is moist and light, with much more flavor than unleavened bread. Any baker knows it just takes a small amount to bring about this wonderful change.

Just like the delicious aroma of fresh bread fills up a kitchen or the neighborhood around a bakery, in the same way the influence of the kingdom of God expressed through us should permeate the lost and dying world around us and bring lost people to Jesus, "the Bread of Life" (John 6:35).

QUICK QUIZ

1. The study of metals and their properties is called _____. (Fill in the blank.)

2. Scandium is currently being studied to see if it should be used in the aerospace industry to reinforce what metal used to build aircraft?

   a. steel   b. aluminum   c. tungsten   d. tin

3. What percentage of scandium is needed to reinforce the metal used to make airplane bodies?

   a. less than 1 percent   b. 10 percent   c. 20 percent   d. 30 percent

4. Scandium reinforcement allows airplane bodies to be _____ together instead of riveted together.

   a. screwed   b. glued   c. welded   d. fastened

5. What is the substance that causes bread to rise?

RESPONSE

Leaven also has negative aspects in the New Testament. In Matthew 16:6–12, Jesus warned His followers against the "leaven of the Pharisees" (Jewish legalism), and in 1 Corinthians 5:6, Paul warns that moral corruption can penetrate the Church just like leaven.

"Heavenly Father, thank You for Your providence. Just like leaven lifts and gives flavor to bread, help me to be a good influence in my world and a good representative of Your Kingdom. Thank You for sending the Bread of Life, Your Son, Jesus. In His name I pray. Amen."

TITANIUM: "The Strongest of Metals"

"There were giants on the earth in those days . . ." (Gen. 6:4).

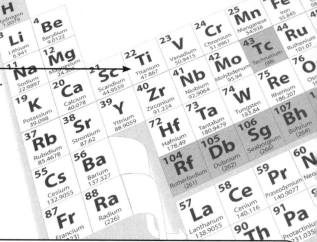

DATA

> In 1791 Rev. William Gregor discovered a mineral that contained a metal that was later named titanium by the German chemist Martin Heinrich Klaproth. Pure titanium was not isolated until 1910.

> Titanium is the ninth most abundant element in the earth's crust and the seventh most abundant metal.

> Until World War II, it was rarely used since it was difficult to work with. However, new technology has made it more common and less expensive.

> Its name was taken from the ancient "Titans," mighty giants who sprang from the earth in Greek myths.

> Titanium has the highest "strength-to-mass" ratio of any metal, meaning it is the strongest metal based on its weight. Titanium shares its strength with other metals when it is alloyed with them.

ANALYSIS

Reverend William Gregor was the pastor in the town of Cornwall, England. While he was a beloved and respected minister to his parishioners, Gregor was a man of many interests, including painting, etching, and music. But his favorite hobby was mineralogy. He had no formal science education but eventually earned quite a reputation in the field. His most lasting discovery was a mineral that he found near his church, a gray-black magnetic sand that looked a lot like gunpowder. After much study, Gregor concluded that this mineral was probably a mixture of iron oxide and the oxide of a new unknown metal.

Later, a German chemist, Martin Heinrich Klaproth, verified that Gregor's mineral did in fact contain a new metal. Klaproth was a respected scientist, but he insisted on giving credit for the element's discovery to the amateur Gregor. However, Klaproth claimed the privilege of naming the new element for his own. He called it "titanium," after the Titans, the ancient giants of Greek mythology. This was not because he believed the new metal would have any special qualities. The Titans were said to have been born "from the earth," and Klaproth thought this new metal derived from the earth should be named after them.

TITANIUM TODAY

Although Klaproth had no way of knowing this, it turns out that titanium is quite "titanic." It is a metal with many special properties: 1) Based on its weight, titanium is the strongest of all metals. For example pure titanium is 45 percent lighter than steel but just as strong. 2) Titanium is highly resistant to corrosion, and it can be used to store very powerful acids. 3) Titanium is totally non-poisonous to the human body. 4) Finally, titanium alloys easily with other metals and it can share its titanic properties with them.

AEROSPACE AND MARINE. Alloys of titanium with aluminum, vanadium, or other metals are used increasingly in aircraft, ships, and spacecraft due to their light weight, strength, and durability. Titanium is used in deep-sea vessels to resist the crushing pressure of the depths.

MEDICAL. Titanium is strong, light, non-toxic, and not rejected by the human body. This makes it a perfect material for dental or surgical implants (such as plates and screws to repair fractures, and even artificial hips), which can remain safely in the body for 30 years or more.

CONSUMER PRODUCTS. Titanium was once considered an exotic metal due to the difficulty of producing it, but new processes have made titanium and its alloys increasingly common. Titanium is used to make stronger and lighter tennis rackets, golf clubs, and bicycles. More and more applications for the strongest metal continue to be found: from tools and firearms to cookware and jewelry. And most horsemen agree, from Amish buggy drivers to horse racers, titanium makes the best horseshoes you can buy!

Titanium has truly become the "giant" of metals.

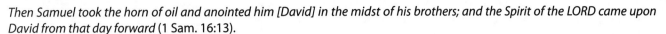

REACTION: *FACING YOUR GIANTS*

Then Samuel took the horn of oil and anointed him [David] in the midst of his brothers; and the Spirit of the LORD came upon David from that day forward (1 Sam. 16:13).

David faced many challenges in his life, but the biggest one was Goliath. This Philistine titan stood over nine feet tall. For 40 days, Goliath mocked God and the armies of Israel. Even Saul, the great warrior-king, was afraid to face him. David was just a young shepherd, but when he heard of Goliath's blasphemous attacks, he decided he had to do something. He asked, "Who is this uncircumcised Philistine, that he should defy the armies of the living God?" (1 Sam. 17:26).

Now David had relied on God's help many times in the past to protect his flocks from wild animals. "The LORD, who delivered me from the paw of the lion and from the paw of the bear, He will deliver me from the hand of this Philistine" (1 Sam. 17:37). He knew that God was the source of his strength. "For You have armed me with strength for the battle" (Ps. 18:39).

Relying on God, David faced Goliath and defeated him. As he approached the giant, David called out, "You come to me with a sword, with a spear, and with a javelin. But I come to you in the name of the LORD of hosts, the God of the armies of Israel, whom you have defied" (1 Sam. 17:45).

With God on his side, David defeated the titanic force of his enemy.

QUICK QUIZ

1. Titanium is the _____ metal based on its weight.

   a. hardest   b. heaviest   c. most reactive   d. strongest

2. Which of the following is *not* a property of titanium that makes it ideal for surgical and dental implants?

   a. non-toxic   b. not rejected by the body   c. lightweight   d. silvery color

3. When titanium is mixed with other metals it forms _____ _____.

   a. magnetic sand   b. strong alloys   c. clear solids   d. powerful acids

4. Which of the following does *not* apply to the biblical description of Goliath?

   a. 9 feet tall   b. Jewish   c. Philistine   d. giant

5. William Gregor of England discovered titanium, but he was not a trained scientist. What was William Gregor's occupation?

RESPONSE

"Lord, You are the same God who strengthened David. You are mightier than any giant that I face in my life. Like David, I will put my trust in You and sing songs of praise to You. Amen."

VANADIUM: "Treasures in Heaven"

*"But lay up for yourselves treasures in heaven, where neither moth nor **rust** destroys and where thieves do not break in and steal"* (Matt. 6:20, emphasis added).

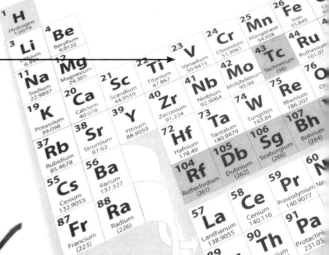

DATA

> Vanadium was first discovered in Mexico in 1801 by Andres del Rio, a Spanish mineralogist, but other scientists convinced him that it was merely chromium, a similar metal (next to vanadium on the periodic table) that had been discovered years earlier.

> In 1830 it was re-discovered by the Swedish chemist Nils G. Sefström. The fashion of the day was to name new elements after Greek mythological characters. But as a proud Scandinavian, Sefstrom named his discovery after the beautiful Norse goddess Vanadis.

> Vanadium is a bright, white metal, which is very resistant to corrosion

> Although it has many industrial uses, over 80 percent of vanadium produced is used to make tough, corrosion resistant forms of steel: much of it for tools.

ANALYSIS

Iron is first mentioned in the Bible all the way back in Genesis 4:22, which describes Tubal-Cain as a craftsman who worked "in brass and iron." Later the Israelites also knew how to work with iron (Deut. 4:20; 1 Kings 8:51, etc.), probably having learned from the Egyptians during their captivity there.

For as long as the metal has been used, mankind has had to guard against iron's great natural enemy: rust. Iron tools had to be kept clean and dry; otherwise they would corrode and rapidly become useless. Iron's use as a building material is limited to applications where it will not be exposed to moisture. Jesus even mentioned the problem of "rust" in the Sermon on the Mount (Matt. 6:19–20).

Over the centuries, man has learned to combat rust in a number of ways. Sometimes iron and steel are galvanized (covered with a layer of zinc) to prevent rusting. This is especially useful for fasteners, like nails and screws. For sheet steel, like cans and ductwork, a coating of tin is often applied. Chrome-plating is often used as a more decorative means of rust-proofing for automobiles and furniture. But none of these coatings (zinc, tin, or chromium) is tough enough for tools like wrenches and hammers, which require a more durable metal.

Throughout history, a good craftsman had to conscientiously care for his iron and steel tools. They had to be cleaned after each use and wiped down with an oily rag. A liberal coating of oil was the best prevention against moisture in the air that could damage a worker's tools in a short time. Well-oiled tools stored neatly in a clean toolbox were often the mark of a good workman.

But in the late 20th century, vanadium-steel became an increasingly common material for tool-making. Due to its special properties, the addition of small amounts of vanadium (as little as 0.05 to 0.15 percent) to regular steel makes tools that are extremely resistant to corrosion, heat, and wear. Also, vanadium makes steel stronger, so tools can be made thinner and lighter without sacrificing strength. Vanadium also makes tools shiny and easy to clean.

Vanadium is largely responsible for the striking difference in the appearance of the tools in your grandfather's toolbox and your father's.

REACTION: *WHERE NEITHER MOTH NOR RUST DESTROYS*

The religious leaders of Jesus' day, the Pharisees, put great emphasis on material blessings as signs of God's approval. They were the "upper class." Some of them figured that since they had fine clothes, nice homes, and riches, they must have been doing something right. God must be on their side. They took pride in their possessions and looked down on the poor as "unclean." (An illustration of this prideful attitude can be found in Luke 18:10–14.)

But in Matthew 6:19–21, Jesus told these proud people that their material blessings or "earthly treasures" were only temporary. Their clothes could be eaten by "moths." Chariots (like cars) would "rust" away. And even more durable possessions like gold and silver can be taken by "thieves." Jesus told them to lay up their "treasures in heaven" where they would be safe in God's hands.

WHAT ARE HEAVENLY TREASURES?

They are the rewards that God has prepared for His servants. In describing these rewards, Paul says "Eye has not seen, nor ear heard, nor have entered into the heart of man the things which God has prepared for those who love Him" (1 Cor. 2:9).

HOW DO WE EARN THESE REWARDS THAT WILL LAST FOREVER?

Paul put it succinctly in his instructions to Timothy, who was pastor of the church at Ephesus. You might consider this Paul's "Eternal Life Insurance Policy":

> *Command those who are rich in this present age not to be haughty, nor to trust in uncertain riches but in the living God, who gives us richly all things to enjoy. Let them do good, that they be rich in good works, ready to give, willing to share, storing up for themselves a good foundation for the time to come, that they may lay hold on eternal life* (1 Tim. 6:17–19).

QUICK QUIZ

1. When vanadium was first discovered in 1801 in Mexico, it was confused with what other metal?

   a. scandium   b. aluminum   c. chromium   d. iron

2. The corrosion of iron is often referred to as _____. (Fill in the blank.)

3. Besides vanadium, all of the following metals are used to help iron resist corrosion, except:

   a. zinc   b. chromium   c. sodium   d. tin

4. Steel protected by a layer of zinc is referred by what adjective?

5. In the Sermon on the Mount, Jesus told His followers that they should store up "treasures _____ _____."
   (Fill in the blanks.)

RESPONSE

"Lord, I know that everything I entrust to You will be protected, from moths and rust and thieves. I will lay up my treasures in heaven, where You can keep them safely in Your hands."

CHROMIUM: "An Element of Many Colors"

"No mention shall be made of coral or quartz; for the price of wisdom is above rubies" (Job 28:18).

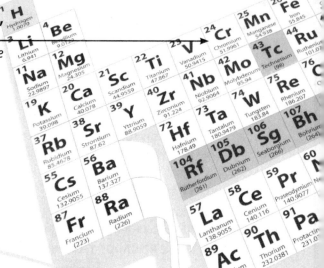

DATA

> Chromium is a very hard, silvery metal with a blue tinge. It was discovered by the French chemist L.N. Vauquelin in 1797. (Vauquelin was also the discoverer of beryllium, element 5.)

> Vauquelin named his element after the Greek word *chroma*, meaning "color," after discovering that many chromium compounds are vividly colored.

> Later it was discovered that the red color of rubies was caused by trace amounts of chromic oxide (Cr_2O_3) as an impurity in alumina (AlO_2).

> Chromium is mainly used to chrome-plate steel (like the bumpers and trim of classic cars) and to make stainless steel, a corrosion-resistant form of steel.

ANALYSIS

Louis Nicolas Vauquelin was born to French peasants. He was a bright teenager, and at age 14 he became a pharmacist's assistant. He had to flee Paris during the French Revolution (to escape the guillotine!), but he eventually returned and became an accomplished chemist and the director of mines for France. In that position, he studied many minerals. One of these was an ore from Russia that was literally worth its weight in gold: "Siberian red lead." It was very popular as a red pigment for oil paints, and in 18th-century Europe, there was a great demand for brilliant colors. Vauquelin knew the ore contained some lead, but he knew something else caused the mineral's rich red color. He wanted to find out its true chemical makeup.

HOW CHROMIUM GOT ITS NAME

In 1796 Vauquelin began a series of experiments that revealed the many colors of chromium.

First, he boiled some of the so-called Siberian red lead in a solution of potassium carbonate. This caused the lead portion to separate out as a precipitate and left behind a bright yellow liquid, containing a mineral he had never seen before. When he added a tin compound to the yellow solution, it turned green. Later he mixed in a mercury solution, which caused a beautiful red solid to form. Eventually he discovered that blue and purple compounds of this element could be formed as well.

After working with these compounds for a whole year, Vauquelin was finally able to produce pure chromium metal. Now convinced that he had discovered a new element, he discussed what its name should be with some friends. They suggested chromium (for the Greek word *chroma,* meaning "color") because of the many colors he had been able to draw out of the mystery element. So "chromium" it was!

Vauquelin later analyzed emeralds and discovered that their green color is caused by the presence of trace amounts of chromium. Still later it was discovered that rubies also get their redness from chromium, the element of many colors.

REACTION: *THE SYMBOL OF WISDOM*

Corundum (a form of alumina, Al_2O_3) is a very hard mineral that is used to make sandpaper.

It is common and inexpensive. However, corundum is occasionally found with an "impurity" called chromic oxide (Cr_2O_3). A tiny amount of this chromium compound makes the grayish, translucent, nearly worthless corundum rock into a brilliant red ruby, one of the most expensive gemstones. For that reason it has been said that chromium (as chromic oxide) is the most valuable substance in the world . . . when purchased in the form of a ruby.

The beautiful red ruby seemed to represent spiritual wisdom to the writers of the Bible, perhaps due to its great value. Job said, "For the price of wisdom is above rubies" (Job 28:18).

In the Proverbs, godly wisdom is often personified as a female.

Happy is the man who finds wisdom. . . . She is more precious than rubies, and all the things you may desire cannot compare with her (Prov. 3:13–15; also see Prov. 8:11).

There is gold and a multitude of rubies, but the lips of knowledge are a precious jewel (Prov. 20:15).

And finally, a wise wife is more precious than any jewels:

Who can find a virtuous wife? For her worth is far above rubies. The heart of her husband safely trusts her; so he will have no lack of gain (Prov. 31:10–11).

QUICK QUIZ

1. The Greek word for "color" is _____.

2. What gem receives its green color from chromium?

    a. emerald   b. topaz   c. aquamarine   d. turquoise

3. In the Bible, rubies represent _____ (Fill in the blank.)

4. Louis Nicolas Vauquelin was the French chemist who discovered chromium. Vauquelin had to flee his homeland to escape what historical event?

5. The use of chromium to make steel surfaces (like old car bumpers) shiny and reflective is called _____ _____. (Fill in the blanks.)

RESPONSE

"Heavenly Father, You have given us the rainbow and all of its colors as a reminder of Your covenant with us. Lord, let my faith in You be as enduring and valuable as a precious gem that dazzles the eye and amazes the heart. Lead me to true wisdom that is worth more than anything that I, in my carnal heart, can desire. Amen."

25
Mn
54.938

MANGANESE: "Iron's Next-Door Neighbor"

"For all the law is fulfilled in one word, even in this: 'You shall love your neighbor as yourself'" (Gal. 5:14).

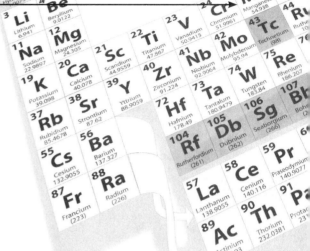

DATA

> Manganese is a hard, brittle, grayish white metal.

> Manganese oxide (MnO) is the tenth most abundant compound in the earth's crust.

> The name manganese comes from Magnesia, a mineral-rich region of Greece. The words "magnesium" and "magnet" also come from Magnesia.

> In 1774 the Swedish chemist Carl Scheele recognized manganese as a new element, and his fellow Swede Johan Gottlieb Gahn first isolated it in 1775.

> Manganese has many properties similar to iron, its neighboring element in the periodic table.

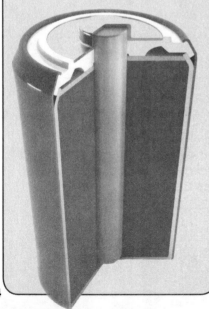

ANALYSIS

Manganese is a metal that most people are unfamiliar with. It is often confused with magnesium, a very different metal. Yet manganese is the fourth most used metal in the world, ranked just behind iron, aluminum, and copper. Americans come into contact with it daily without even realizing it. Manganese helps make many of the objects in our daily lives, including batteries, aluminum cans, and electronics. But the most important role manganese plays in modern life is in the production of steel, by teaming up with its next-door neighbor, iron.

MANGANESE STEEL. The secret history of manganese began in the Iron Age, a time when iron replaced bronze for making tools and weapons. Due to its similarity to iron, manganese was not recognized as a separate metal until 1774, but it is present in most iron ore deposits in various amounts. And in ancient Greece, manganese may have changed history.

As the knowledge of iron-making grew, it was learned that adding a little carbon to iron made the metal harder (i.e., man learned to make steel). Soon blacksmiths all over the ancient world were making steel weapons. But some areas produced better steel than others. Spartan steel became well known for making excellent swords that kept their sharpness and did not break easily in battle. This high-quality steel helped to make the Greek city of Sparta the dominant force in the 7th century B.C. Modern analysis of Greek iron mines confirms that the presence of high manganese levels was responsible for Sparta's superior weapons.

We now know that increasing the carbon content of steel increases its hardness but makes it brittle. However, adding manganese increases steel's hardness, without reducing its malleability or toughness. Today about 95 percent of the world's annual production of manganese is used by the steel industry.

MANGANESE AND IRON IN HEALTH. Both iron and manganese are essential to almost all living things, from bacteria to humans. In humans, iron is mostly found in the blood and manganese is found mostly in the bones. Manganese's importance in bone growth is not well understood, but lack of it leads to bone diseases. Both minerals are required for metabolism and the proper function of various enzymes.

Throughout history, the elemental neighbors, iron and manganese working together, have contributed to human technology and health. This reminds us of the biblical proverb: "As iron sharpens iron, so a man sharpens the countenance of his friend" (Prov. 27:17).

REACTION: *WHO IS MY NEIGHBOR?*

He who despises his neighbor sins (Prov. 14:21).

As Jesus' popularity grew, many sincere people came to Him for spiritual guidance. But some came with trick questions. They were critics who wanted to trick Jesus into giving an unpopular answer or one that contradicted the Hebrew Scriptures. The Bible calls them "lawyers," but they were not attorneys or legal advocates, as we think of them today. They were men who were trained in the complexities of Jewish Law.

One of these lawyers asked Jesus a question: How do I receive eternal life? The Bible says this lawyer was "testing" Him. Jesus perceived that the man was an expert in the Law, so He turned the question around. "What does the Law say?" He asked. The man quoted the Old Testament and gave a two-fold answer: love the Lord (from Deut. 6:5) and love your neighbor as yourself (from Lev. 19:18). Jesus said the lawyer answered well.

But this wasn't good enough for the man. He wanted to know: "Who is my neighbor?" In other words, is it the guy next door? The neighbor down the street? Or is it anyone in my hometown? Just who do I have to love to get into heaven?

Jesus gave him the broadest answer He could. He told him a story about a traveler who had been robbed, beaten, stripped, and left for dead. Soon a priest came by, but he did not help the poor man. Another religious man, a Levite, passed by as well. These "men of God" loved the Lord, perhaps, but they were too busy to be bothered with the injured man's care. So by the Law's standard, they were unworthy of heaven.

Fortunately for the victim, a third man came along: a Samaritan. Jesus said the Samaritan had compassion on the man. He gave him first aid, then put the man on his own horse and walked him to a nearby inn, where he cared for him all night long. The next day, the Samaritan had to leave, but he paid the innkeeper to care for the injured man until he could return.

In those days, the Jews and Samaritans disliked, even hated, each other. The prejudice was like racism with deep religious overtones. But Jesus was saying that this despised Samaritan was more worthy of heaven than the two Jewish holy men. This was probably hard for the lawyer to take.

Then Jesus asked the lawyer, "Which of the these three do you think was neighbor to him that fell among the thieves?" The lawyer answered correctly: "He who showed mercy." Yet the lawyer could not bring himself to use the word Samaritan. Jesus ended the discussion simply by saying, "Go and do likewise." (The story of the Good Samaritan is found in Luke 10:25–37.)

QUICK QUIZ

1. Manganese is the fourth most used metal in the world, based on the amount produced each year. Which of the following metals is not in the top three?

   a. iron   b. copper   c. nickel   d. aluminum

2. In ancient Greece, the steel from a certain region contained high levels of manganese. This steel made stronger weapons. What city of Greece had this sturdy form of steel?

   a. Ephesus   b. Corinth   c. Philippi   d. Sparta

3. Which part of your body contains the most manganese?

   a. bones   b. blood   c. eyes   d. skin

4. Ninety-five percent of the world's production of manganese is used by the _____ industry. (Fill in the blank.)

5. Jesus' parable of "The Good Samaritan" (from Luke 10) was a lesson on how to treat one's _____.

   a. friends   b. enemies   c. relatives   d. neighbors

RESPONSE

When a neighbor is in need, God expects us to do what we can to help him or her, not to wait on the government or the church or the next person who comes along.

When God puts someone in our path who needs help, we are not to look down on him or her as beneath us. The example of the Samaritan makes it clear. Even if it delays our schedule, gets us dirty, or costs us personally, God expects us to treat the person in need like a neighbor.

"Lord, help me to show love to my neighbor wherever I find him. May I learn to love like Christ! Amen."

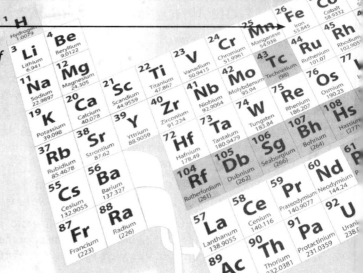

26
Fe
55.845

IRON: "The Element of Salvation"

"Now out of His mouth goes a sharp sword, that with it he should strike the nations. And He Himself will rule them with a rod of iron" (Rev. 19:15).

DATA

> Iron has been used since antiquity. It is the fourth most abundant element in the earth's surface.

> Iron is a silvery gray metal, but it oxidizes readily to rust (iron oxide or Fe_2O_3).

> Iron is from an Old English word, *iren*. The symbol Fe is from the Latin word for iron, *ferrum*.

> Iron forms the heart of the hemoglobin molecule, which allows blood to carry oxygen to the cells of our bodies. The iron in hemoglobin also makes blood red.

ANALYSIS

Iron is mentioned over 90 times in the Bible. It is named as one of the first metals ever to be worked by man in Genesis 4:22. ("Tubal-Cain [was] an instructor of every craftsman in bronze and iron.") Later, when the Israelites were held as slaves in Egypt, along with brick-making, they were forced to work in the smelting of iron. ("But the LORD has taken you and brought you forth out of the iron furnace, even out of Egypt . . ." [Deut. 4:20].)

After the Exodus, the Jews took that iron-making ability with them into the Promised Land. The Bible tells us they had iron weapons in Numbers 35:16. Joshua and his followers defeated the Canaanites with weapons of iron and occupied the land (Josh. 11:10, etc.).

But the Israelites eventually lost their iron-making skills. In the time of Samson (Judg. 13:1), Israel was invaded and conquered by the Philistines, in part due to their advanced knowledge of metallurgy. First Samuel 13:19–22 tells us that there was not even one smith in all of Israel at that time. The Philistine domination of the Jews continued until the time of David. In 1 Samuel 17, when David faced Goliath, the head of the giant's spear was said to be made of iron and weighed 20 pounds! (See verse 7.) With God's help, young David used a sling and stone to defeat the superior technology of the Philistine.

Later, David became king. He and his armies defeated the Philistines, and they regained the metallurgical knowledge they had lost in previous centuries.

THE CARPENTER'S SON: TOOLS AND NAILS

The New Testament tells us that Jesus was both a carpenter (Mark 6:3) and the son of a carpenter (Matt. 13:55), so Jesus was well acquainted with tools of iron, such as saws, squares, chisels, and planes. And of course, He was familiar with nails.

The last mention of iron in the Bible comes in the Book of Revelation where we are told that when He returns, Christ will rule with "a rod of iron," which He will use to break Satan and all the forces of evil (Rev. 12:5, 19:15).

THE BLOOD OF THE LAMB

The Hebrew writer said that the blood of bulls and goats could not save us from our sins (Heb. 10:4). Only the blood of the perfect Lamb of God (John 1:29) shed on the Cross was an acceptable sacrifice: blood made red by the iron of hemoglobin. In many ways, iron is the element of our salvation.

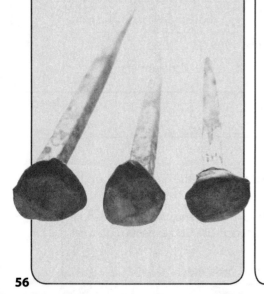

REACTION: *WITHOUT THE SHEDDING OF BLOOD...*

Almost all things are by the law purged with blood; and without shedding of blood there is no remission (Heb. 9:22; KJV).

Of all of the elements, iron is most associated with salvation.

With an axe of iron, a tree was felled. With the iron tools of a carpenter, the wood was shaped into beams, and the beams were made into the form of a cross that Jesus carried through the streets of Jerusalem. With a whip, tipped with bits of bone and iron, Christ was scourged to satisfy the angry mob. ("By whose stripes you were healed" [1 Pet. 2:24].)

With a heavy iron mallet, three iron nails were driven through Christ's flesh and into the hard wood of the cross. Finally, with the iron tip of a spear, a Roman soldier pierced the Savior's side, and blood and water flowed out. ("We have redemption through His blood" [Eph. 1:7].)

Without the shedding of blood there is no remission (Heb. 9:22). This is the central doctrine of Christianity. Iron was the means of our salvation.

The Bible tells us that God's plan for saving us from our sins by the shedding of the blood of Jesus Christ was established at the beginning. God knew that His only begotten Son would have to give His life on the Cross. When God created the world on the first day, He planted the elements in the earth's skin and spread the ores of metal in its veins. He put many iron mines in Israel.

God made iron soft enough to be pounded into the shape of a nail by a blacksmith; hard enough to pierce skin, flesh, and tendons; and durable enough to hold the Savior on the cross until our salvation was accomplished. ("[Jesus] said, 'It is finished!' And bowing His head, He gave up His spirit" [John 19:30].)

QUICK QUIZ

1. What biblical character was the first person described as a "craftsman in bronze and iron" (Gen. 4:22)?

    a. David   b. Joshua   c. Tubal-Cain   d. Samson

2. The Israelites probably learned how to smelt iron when they were held as slaves in what country?

3. What is the chemical name for rust?

4. What iron-based molecule in red blood cells makes blood red?

5. According to Hebrews 9:22, "Without the shedding of blood, there is no _____."

    a. forgiveness   b. righteousness   c. remission   d. neighbor

RESPONSE

The next time you hold a nail in your hand, take a moment to ponder its origin. Feel the sharpness of its point. Notice its hardness and length. Think about the purpose of the flat head.

How many nails did Jesus handle in His time on earth? How many did He pound into wooden beams? Yet He knowingly went to the cross "for the joy that was set before Him" (Heb. 12:2). That's how much He loves us.

"Heavenly Father, thank You for providing a means of salvation for sinners like me — the perfect sacrifice that makes it possible for me to commune with You. I pray that I never take my salvation for granted, because I know that it cost You the world. Every nail I see is a reminder of Your love for me. In Jesus' name. Amen."

27
Co
58.9332

COBALT: "Goblins and Demons"

"Now the Spirit expressly says that in latter times some will depart from the faith, giving heed to deceiving spirits and doctrines of demons" (1 Tim. 4:1).

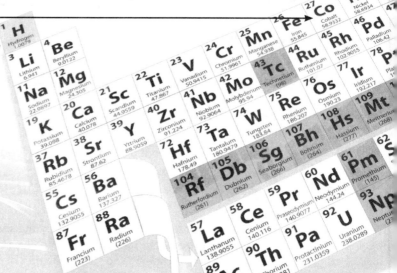

DATA

> Cobalt is a silvery-white, brittle metal with a slight bluish tint.

> Cobalt is used mostly in magnetic applications. Like iron, it is easily magnetized and it maintains its magnetism at higher temperatures than any other alloy or metal.

> One-fourth of the world's production of cobalt is used to make alnico, a "supermagnetic" alloy of aluminum, nickel, and cobalt.

> Cobalt was discovered in about 1737 by the Swedish metallurgist Georg Brandt.

> Cobalt provides the key element in vitamin B-12.

> Cobalt is the English spelling of the German name for the element, *kobalt.*

ANALYSIS

Copper has been mined in and around Germany since at least the 10th century. In the Middle Ages, there was a German superstition about little subterranean mine-demons called "kobalds." The miners believed these kobalds would come up from deep in the earth to play tricks on them. Sometimes the mischievous creatures would destroy equipment or lead miners in wrong directions. The kobalds also left false ores in the mines. In the churches in many medieval mining towns, the people held special prayer services for deliverance from these pesky pests.

A PROBLEMATIC ORE

There was a troublesome ore that was found in many copper mines. The miners disliked it because it was considered worthless. It was labor intensive to remove in order to get to profitable ores. And often it was contaminated with arsenic dust, which affected the health of the miners. With all the problems this unwanted ore caused, it was no wonder the miners referred to it by the name of their pesky underground enemies. They called this bad ore *kobald.*

Eventually uses were found even for this problematic ore. In the 15th century German glassmakers found that the ore gave a beautiful blue color to glass and pottery. They began to export their blue-tinted glass all over Europe. Later the ore was used for "bluing," a laundry chemical that make clothes look whiter. The ore was also used to make blue ink.

When Georg Brandt, a Swedish chemist, was 33, he was placed in charge of the Bureau of Mines in Stockholm, in 1727. Among his many contributions to chemistry was his study of the so-called kobald ore. Brandt was able to isolate a previously unknown metal in it. He named this new metallic element kobalt for the mineral from which he derived it. In English, it became cobalt, and blue-tinted glass is now referred to as "cobalt blue."

(The myth of the kobalds has persisted for many centuries. Believe it or not, it even survives in modern American culture in a modified form. The word kobald entered into the English language: with a few spelling changes, it became our word "goblin." So remember the kobalds of the old German miners next Halloween when you are passing out treats to the neighborhoods' goblins.)

REACTION: *THE DARKNESS OF THIS AGE*

For we do not wrestle against flesh and blood, but against principalities, against powers, against the rulers of the darkness of this age, against spiritual hosts of wickedness in the heavenly places (Eph. 6:12).

The miners believed that they encountered the mine demons because they were intruding into the demon's home territory. They believed that as they penetrated the darkness of the mines, the kobalds fought back against them. As in many superstitious beliefs, this one may contain an element of truth.

In the Bible, demons were mostly encountered when the people of God actively took the light of the gospel into the darkness of the world. (See Acts 26:17–18.) Jesus encountered evil spirits and healed many demon-possessed people during His earthly ministry. He said that His disciples would be able cast out demons as well (Mark 16:17). In fact, the Apostles frequently faced demonic resistance as they took the gospel into pagan lands. (See Acts 8:6–8, 16:16–18, and 19:11–12). Missionaries in primitive lands encounter resistance from demonic forces as they spread the Word. They must rely on God for His protection and to help them in delivering those possessed by demons.

Even though their influence may not be as obvious, demons and the forces of darkness are active in modern society as well. Addiction to drugs and alcohol, pornography, and other perversions are often connected to demonic influence. (See Eph. 6:12.) In the realms of the media and higher education, even in the government, many influential people of our society have subscribed to what the Bible calls "doctrines of demons" (1 Tim. 4:1). These doctrines have led to the rejection of God, acceptance of evolutionary beliefs, and the debasement of the family, among other evils.

QUICK QUIZ

1. Cobalt and certain alloys of cobalt are used to make powerful _____.

    a. magnets   b. acids   c. drugs   d. explosives

2. Cobalt imparts a _____ tint to glass.

    a. yellow   b. red   c. green   d. blue

3. Cobalt ore often contains high levels of what poisonous element?

4. Cobalt is the key element in what vitamin?

    a. A   b. B-6   c. B-12   d. C

5. Superstitious German miners in the Middle Ages believed in supernatural mine-spirits that they called "_____."

    a. ghosts   b. gremlins   c. ogres   d. kobalds

RESPONSE

In his letter to the Romans, Paul says to "put on the armor of light" to resist the forces of darkness:

> *The night is far spent, the day is at hand. Therefore let us cast off the works of darkness, and let us put on the armor of light* (Rom. 13:12).

"Father, thank You for Jesus, the Light of the World. I will spread the gospel as You have told us. I promise to keep myself under Your protection, the armor of light, to stand up against the forces of the devil. Light my path in the darkness. Amen."

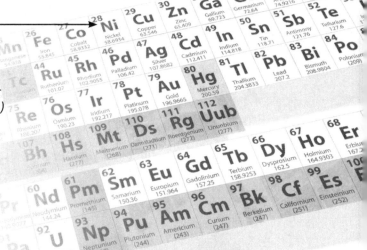

28
Ni
58.6934

NICKEL: "The Devil's Ore"

"Iron is taken from the earth, and copper is smelted from ore. Man puts an end to darkness, and searches every recess for ore in the darkness and the shadow of death" (Job 28:2–3) (A description of the work of miners is found in Job 28:1–11.)

DATA

> Nickel is described as a silvery, lustrous metal with a slight gold tinge. Nickel is hard and ductile.

> Pure nickel was first isolated by the Swedish mineralogist Axel Fredrik Cronstedt (1722–1765) in Sweden in 1751.

> Nickel is resistant to oxidation, so it is often used (as an alloy) in coins.

> Nickel's most common use is in alloys.

> The U.S. nickel coin is 75 percent copper and 25 percent nickel. The actual value of metal in a nickel is about 10 cents as of the year 2008. (3.75 grams of copper: 3.5 cents; 1.25 grams of nickel, 6.5 cents.)

> Pure nickel is magnetic, but U.S. nickels are not magnetic due to the copper concentration.

> Nickel's name is a shortened version of an old German name of an ore that miners called *kupfernickel*.

ANALYSIS

Some elements are named after mythical gods and goddesses: mercury, uranium, palladium, etc. Others are named for scientists of the past: curium, einsteinium, fermium, and others. Some, like scandium, ytterbium, and magnesium, are named for the places where they were first found. But one particular element, one that most Americans come into contact with every day, is actually named after the devil!

HOW NICKEL GOT ITS NAME. Throughout history there have been several professions known for their superstitions. Like soldiers and sailors, miners felt that they were especially subject to forces beyond their control: forces of gods or spirits. To a mineworker, every day of labor and every new shaft held the potential for death. Superstitious miners sought out various deities and "earth spirits" for safety in the mines and to lead them to good seams of minerals. And for protection from bad spirits.

Copper ore has been mined in and around Germany since at least the 10th century. While copper was very valuable, mineworkers frequently encountered ores that were almost indistinguishable from true copper ore, yet they produced no copper. They called these worthless ores "kupfernickel," which in English translates as "Old Nick's copper." Old Nick was the miners' name for the devil. It was their belief that Satan placed this "false ore" in the mines to cause them to waste their time and to lead them in dangerous directions. (Compare this to cobalt's story, element 27.)

THE USEFULNESS OF NICKEL. As we now know, nickel is hardly a worthless material. European glassmakers discovered the first major use for nickel compounds (as they did for cobalt compounds): nickel ore could be used to impart a green tint to glass.

In modern metallurgy, nickel lends its corrosion resistance to other metals in many alloys, such as Monel, Hastelloy, and types of stainless steel. Nickel alloys are used extensively in desalination plants to resist the corrosiveness of seawater. It is also used to make some types of magnets.

Finally, nickel is also required in the human body as a trace element. Nickel atoms are at the hearts of several key enzymes required for good health. It is present in all of our tissues and blood. And it regulates various body processes.

REACTION: *THE DECEIVER OF THE WHOLE WORLD*

So the great dragon was cast out, that serpent of old, called the Devil and Satan, who deceives the whole world; he was cast to the earth, and his angels were cast out with him (Rev. 12:9).

Be sober, be vigilant; because your adversary the devil walks about like a roaring lion, seeking whom he may devour (1 Pet. 5:8).

The miners described on page 60 believed the devil, or Old Nick as they called him, distracted them with false ores that would lead them away from their true goal. The devil has been a deceiver and tempter from the beginning.

Satan first appeared in the Garden of Eden, where he deceived Eve regarding the character and nature of God, and tempted her with forbidden fruit (Gen. 3). Satan was the adversary who oppressed Job and tried to get him to curse God (Job 1:11). Also, Satan tempted David to take a census that God had forbidden (1 Chron. 21:1).

Satan's ultimate temptation was that of Jesus in Matthew 4. He tempted Christ three times, at last offering Him "all the kingdoms of the world and their glory" (Matt. 4:8). The Bible says that Satan is the "god of this world" so the earth's was his to give (2 Cor. 4:4). Christ was weak from 40 days of fasting, and Satan tried to use His weakness to tempt Him to abandon God's plan. His deceptive offer to Jesus was to help Him "save the world" the easy way, rather than to face a gruesome death on the Cross.

But Jesus knew that without the Cross, there would be no salvation and without His own death there would be no resurrection. Jesus rejected the false promises of Satan. "For the joy that was set before Him," He chose the death on the cross (Heb. 12:2).

QUICK QUIZ

1. American five-cent coins are made of 25 percent _____ and 75 percent _____ (as of 2008).

   a. nickel, silver   b. copper, nickel   c. nickel, copper   d. zinc, nickel

2. Nickel imparts a _____ tint to glass.

   a. yellow   b. red   c. blue   d. green

3. Nickel's ability to form corrosion-resistant alloys makes it useful to make all of the following except_____.

   a. coins   b. equipment exposed to seawater   c. car batteries   d. some forms of stainless steel

4. TRUE or FALSE: Nickel is important in the human diet for maintenance of good health.

5. What craftsmen found the first use for nickel?

RESPONSE

"Lord, help me to see though the deceptions of Satan and resist his evil influence. You are the true hope for mankind, and Your Word is a trustworthy guide. Amen."

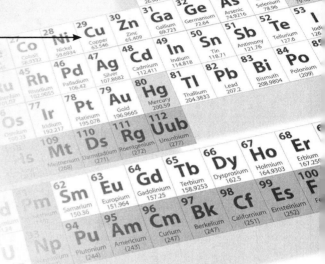

29
Cu
63.546

COPPER: "The Element of Judgment"

"[I gave to the priests] two vessels of fine copper, precious as gold. And I said unto them, Ye are holy unto the LORD; the vessels are holy also" (Ezra 8:27–28).

DATA

> Copper's thermal and electrical conductivity, malleability, and ductility make it uniquely useful for many applications. Other than iron, copper is our most useful metal, as it is used in making pipe, wire, and electrical components.

> Copper is a reddish brown metal. Copper and gold (just below it in the periodic table), along with cesium, are considered to be the only "colored" metals. (All other metals are "white" or "silvery.")

> Historically, copper was alloyed with tin — to make bronze, and later with zinc — to make brass. Both of these alloys are harder and more durable than copper alone.

> Copper mixes well with many metals, and over 1,000 different alloys have been made from it.

> The Romans imported their copper from the island of Cypress. The Latin word for copper, *cuprum*, meant "metal from Cypress," and it is the source for the chemical symbol Cu. In English, *cuprum* became "copper."

ANALYSIS

The word copper appears in the King James Version (KJV) of the Bible only twice (Ezra 8:27; 2 Tim. 4:14). "Brass" (or "brazen") occurs over 100 times, more than any metal except gold and silver. "Bronze" does not appear at all in the KJV, because that word did not come into use until after it was completed. What the KJV calls "brass" is actually what we refer to as bronze today. It was one of the two metals used by the first blacksmith, Tubal-Cain. (See Gen. 4:22.)

For most of human history there were not separate words for copper, brass, and bronze, and the Bible does not distinguish among them. (However, in some verses the form of copper may be inferred from the context.) Pure copper was sometimes available, since it does occur unalloyed in some areas, but bronze was used more commonly. In the following discussion, "bronze" is used for all three forms of copper.

THE USES OF BRONZE IN THE BIBLE. Due to its hardness and workability, bronze appears quite often in the Bible, and it had many uses. Bronze was used for weaponry, such as Goliath's helmet and chain mail (1 Sam. 17:5–6) and the archer's bow in Psalm 18:34 (where the KJV incorrectly uses "steel"). Bronze was also used for coinage. While more valuable coins were made of gold or silver, the most common coins were of bronze. This was the money most used by the poor. (See Element 49, Tin.)

BRONZE USED IN WORSHIP. In the Bible, bronze is the metal most associated with worship and sacrifice. When God told Moses to build a tabernacle in the wilderness (Exod. 26–27), the altar of sacrifice was made of bronze (actually wood covered with bronze). The gate and many other objects used for worship were also bronze. Finally, the large water basin or "laver" in the center of the courtyard, where the Jewish priest washed his hands and feet, was made of polished bronze (Exod. 30:17–22).

Elsewhere in the Bible, other bronze objects related to worship are mentioned. Solomon's temple made extensive use of this alloy (2 Chron. 4). As instructed by the Lord, Moses made a "serpent of bronze" in the wilderness (Num. 21:4–9; John 3:14), and cymbals of bronze were used to celebrate the return of the ark of the covenant to Jerusalem (1 Chron. 15:19).

Finally, in 1 Corinthians 13:1, Paul used the irritating sound of noisy, clanging cymbals to represent faith without love. "Though I speak with the tongues of men and of angels, but have not love, I have become sounding brass or a clanging cymbal." (Here, brass, rather than bronze, may be the appropriate choice. The alloy we now call brass began to be used in Roman times.)

REACTION: *THE TABERNACLE*

The sacrificial death of Jesus Christ on the Cross was exquisitely foreshadowed by the bronze altar of sacrifice in the Jewish tabernacle. Bronze items served several essential functions in the tabernacle.

THE GATE

The gate of the tabernacle consisted of four bronze pillars, hung with purple, blue, scarlet, and white linen. This gate was the only way in. (Jesus said, "I am the door. If anyone enters by Me, he will be saved" [John 10:9].) Through this gate was found forgiveness of sins and the presence of God.

THE ALTAR

Inside the gate was the bronze altar of sacrifice. It was about 7½ feet square with a bronze horn at each corner. In Hebrew, "altar" means "place of slaying" and as such it is the perfect symbol for the cross. The head of the household would place his hand on the sacrificial animal's head, symbolizing the transfer of his own and his family's sin to the innocent creature (Lev. 4:4). The animal was then led in through the gate, where the priest killed it. The blood of the sacrifice was sprinkled in front of the Holy Place and on the horns and base of the altar. "For the life of the flesh is in the blood . . . it is the blood that makes atonement for the soul" (Lev. 17:11). The animal chosen for the sacrifice had to be an unblemished male (typically a lamb), the best the family could afford. The animal symbolized the sinless Lamb of God, Jesus, whose blood was shed to atone for our sins ("the precious blood of Christ, as of a lamb without blemish" [1 Pet. 1:19].)

Then the lamb was placed on the burning altar, and its flesh was roasted. The smoke of the fire rising into the sky reminded the people of the removal of their sins. The meat was then eaten as a reminder that the innocent creature was slain to give them life. On the night before He went to the Cross, Jesus gave His disciples bread and said, "Take, eat; this is My body" (Matt. 26:26). ("Whoever eats My flesh and drinks My blood has eternal life, and I will raise him up at the last day" [John 6:54].)

THE LAVER

Behind the altar was a large bronze laver or washing bowl. When the sacrifice was done, the priest was to wash his hands and feet, both dirty from the bloody sacrifices, before approaching God's presence in the Holy Place (Exod. 30:17–22). This bronze laver was symbolic of man's need for purification before the Lord (see Ps. 24:3; John 13:2–10; 1 John 1:7; etc.) and of baptism (see Acts 2:38, 22:16; etc.).

QUICK QUIZ

1. Bronze is an alloy of copper and _____.

   a. iron   b. tin   c. zinc   d. nickel

2. In the Bible, bronze (or brass in some translations) was used for all of the following except for_____.

   a. coins   b. weapons   c. water pipes   d. objects used in worship

3. Gold, copper, and cesium are the only metals that _____.

   a. are colored   b. conduct heat   c. do not corrode   d. are heavier than lead

4. Which item in the Old Testament tabernacle was not made of bronze (or brass)?

   a. the altar of sacrifice   b. the laver   c. the ark of the covenant   d. the gate

5. In the tabernacle, gold and silver, as pure metals, are believed to represent the purity and holiness of God. But bronze is a mixture of two metals, and it is said to represent the sinfulness and impurity of man. The proper term for a mixture of two or more metals is _____.

   a. isotope   b. fusion   c. compound   d. alloy

RESPONSE

Bronze is not a pure metal, of course. Unlike gold and silver, it is an alloy — essentially impure copper. Bronze symbolizes man's impure nature before God and our need for cleansing. Pure gold, in the form of the ark of the covenant, illustrates God's purity. The priest in the tabernacle needed the ceremonial cleansing of the bronze altar and laver before he could be in the golden presence of God.

30
Zn
65.409

ZINC: "The Element of Protection"

"You are my hiding place; You shall preserve me from trouble; You shall surround me with songs of deliverance. Selah" (Ps. 32:7).

DATA

> Zinc is a lustrous, silvery metal with a bluish tinge. It is brittle at ordinary temperatures but becomes malleable higher than about 210°F (100°C).

> Zinc is believed to come from the Old German word *zink,* meaning "prong," because of zinc's jagged appearance when it cools.

> The German chemist Andreas Marggraf isolated metallic zinc in 1746.

> Brass, the alloy of copper and zinc (typically 30 to 40 percent Zn) has been used extensively since Roman times. (See 1 Cor. 13:1.) The addition of zinc makes brass stronger, more corrosion resistant, and more workable than pure copper.

> Zinc's corrosion resistance is very useful in protecting other metals (especially iron) and this property, as well as zinc's low cost, account for its extensive use as a protective coating.

ANALYSIS

The primary use of zinc is in the "galvanization" of other metals, mainly iron and steel. The process is named after the Italian scientist Luigi Galvani, an early pioneer in the field of electrochemistry. Galvanizing steel involves dipping it in a bath of molten zinc at around 860°F (460°C). The zinc forms a thin protective layer around the steel. Over time, the exposed zinc surface reacts with oxygen, water vapor, and carbon dioxide in the air to form a layer of zinc carbonate ($ZnCO3$). This carbonate layer is insoluble in water, impermeable to air, and adheres tenaciously to the underlying zinc layer. Thus it provides excellent corrosion resistance at a very low cost, since zinc is a cheap metal.

Galvanization with zinc is used to protect many steel products: nails, automobiles, appliances, and structural steel for buildings are just a few. Galvanized steel is used extensively for highway projects. Bridges, guardrail posts, railings, and lamp and sign posts are common examples. The galvanic zinc coating on steel can usually be detected by the blotchy, crystalline pattern on the metal's surface. This pattern is referred to as "spangle" or "spangling."

ANOTHER USE FOR ZINC

In modern life we experience zinc in another form on a daily basis. From 1793 to 1982, the penny has been either pure copper or 95 percent copper in the form of brass or bronze. (The exception was one year during World War II, 1943, when all pennies were made of steel coated with zinc. This was because copper was needed for the war effort.)

As the cost of copper has increased over the years, the government decided to make pennies more cheaply. Since 1982, the U.S. one-cent piece has consisted of a core of 2.4 grams of zinc, coated with 0.6 grams of copper.

As a result, pennies made before 1982 are worth about two cents based on the their metal content, and newer pennies are worth about 0.8 cents (based on 2008 metal prices).

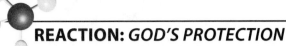

REACTION: *GOD'S PROTECTION*

Many sorrows shall be to the wicked; but he who trusts in the LORD, mercy shall surround him (Ps. 32:10).

The most important use for zinc is to surround iron and steel objects. Exposure to moisture in the environment can be very destructive to bare steel, but a zinc coating protects the metal within from the corrosive effects of nature and keeps the metal strong and long lasting.

This provides an illustration of God's protective influence on our lives. The world we live in can be a harsh place, with storms and hardships. But in Psalm 32 we are promised that the Lord will protect those who honor Him. Verse 6 says, "Surely in a flood of great waters they shall not come near." God is our "hiding place" to shelter us from the storms (verse 7).

When we trust in the Lord, we have God's promise that we will be surrounded by His wonderful mercy (verse 10). Thanks to God's promise of protection we can always "be glad in the LORD and rejoice . . . and shout for joy" (verse 11).

QUICK QUIZ

1. The coating of a metal object (usually iron or steel) with a layer of zinc is called _____. (Fill in the blank.)

2. Galvanized coatings are *not* used in which of the following?

    a. nails   b. bridges   c. cars   d. copper wire

3. The blotchy, irregular, crystal-like pattern that appears on galvanized surfaces is called _____. (Fill in the blank.)

4. The zinc content of U. S. pennies has increased over the years, because:

    a. zinc is cheaper than copper   b. we are running out of copper   c. zinc is heavier than copper   d. the public likes zinc better

5. Zinc protects steel by keeping out _____.

    a. sunlight   b. moisture   c. termites   d. oil

RESPONSE

"Heavenly Father, thank You for Your promise of protection. Whenever the storms and floods of life threaten me, I will always turn to You as my hiding place. Surround me with Your mercy and grace. Amen."

31
Ga
69.723

GALLIUM: "The First Predicted Element"

"Of gold and silver and bronze and iron there is no limit. Arise and begin working, and the LORD be with you"
(1 Chron. 22:16).

DATA

> Gallium is a silvery white metal that is soft enough to be cut with a knife.

> If you held a piece of gallium in your hand, it would soon form a silvery puddle. Its melting point is about 30°C (86°F), which is higher than room temperature but lower than your body temperature.

> Gallium was discovered in 1875 by French chemist Paul-Emile Lecoq de Boisbaudran. He named the element after the Latin word for France, *gallia*. (The name may have a double meaning. For a chemist, Boisbaudran was something of a joker. His middle name, Lecoq, means "the rooster" in French. The Latin word *gallus* means rooster as well, and Boisbaudran joked that he named gallium after himself.)

> Gallium's main uses are in semiconductors and LED (light-emitting diode) applications.

ANALYSIS

Although Paul-Emile de Boisbaudran discovered gallium in 1875, its existence had been predicted in 1869 by the Russian chemist Dmitri Mendeleev as he was developing his periodic table. Mendeleev believed there was a missing element in the space just below aluminum, which he called "eka-aluminum" (meaning "aluminum plus one.") Based on his table, Mendeleev predicted some of the new element's properties.

FRANCE

Boisbaudran's discovery of gallium in a sample of zinc ore just six years later was one of the most significant moments in chemistry. A few of the properties predicted by Mendeleev compared to the actual properties of gallium are presented below:

	PROPERTIES PREDICTED FOR "EKA-ALUMINUM" (Ea) BY MENDELEEV	ACTUAL PROPERTIES OF GALLIUM (Ga) DISCOVERED BY BOISBAUDRAN
Atomic Weight	Approximately 68	69.72
Density	5.9 g/cm³	5.94g/cm³
Solubility	In acids and alkalis	In acids and alkalis
Compounds: Oxide	Ea_2O_3	Ga_2O_3
Chloride	$EaCl_3$	$GaCl_3$

Gallium was the first element predicted by Mendeleev to be discovered. Eventually, seven more would be found: francium, polonium, scandium, technetium, germanium, protactinium, and rhenium.

Before Mendeleev's Table, the elements seemed to be an extremely messy assemblage: a collection of liquids, solids, and gasses, metals and nonmetals, toxic and essential, which could hardly be organized by atomic weight or any other arrangement. It was easy to believe there might be no order to the elements at all. Perhaps they were just a hodgepodge of substances with random properties.

But as the Bible tells us in 1 Corinthians 14:33, "God is not the author of confusion." There is order and purpose in all that God has created, and that includes the elements that comprise our universe. "For since the creation of the world His invisible attributes are clearly seen, being understood by the things that are made, even His eternal power and Godhead, so that they are without excuse" (Rom. 1:20).

In 1887 Mendeleev wrote that in the study of chemistry, his mission was to "patiently search divine and scientific truth." Dmitri Mendeleev's breakthrough was to discover the "divine and scientific truth" in the ordering of the elements.

REACTION: *PROPHETS*

For we know in part and we prophesy in part (1 Cor. 13:9).

Due to his ability to discern recurring patterns among the elements and to order them in a table, Dmitri Mendeleev is revered as a "secular prophet" of chemistry. However, we should note that not all of his prophecies came true. In Mendeleev's time, the structure of the nucleus (made of protons and neutrons) and the orbital arrangements of electrons were still unknown. This incomplete knowledge led Mendeleev to make some wrong predictions. Mendeleev predicted two elements (he called them "ether" and "coronium") that he believed were lighter than hydrogen. Two heavier elements he predicted ("eka-cesium" and "eka-niobium") were wrong as well.

Although the predictions found in the writings of science are often wrong, there is a Book whose predictions are always accurate: the Bible. Scripture contains hundreds of prophecies of historical events that came to pass exactly as the Bible predicted. Many times the prophecy and the fulfillment were centuries apart. The accuracy of these prophecies can only be explained by the divine inspiration of God. No other ancient books or religious writings contain such fulfilled prophecy. The Bible is unique.

And of course, many Bible predictions remain to be realized: including prophecies about Israel and the end times, and especially the return of Christ to earth. The reader is encouraged to study the remarkable record of fulfilled prophecies in the Bible and the promises of blessings to come.

QUICK QUIZ

1. The existence of gallium was predicted by the Russian chemist _____.

   a. Boisbaudran   b. Mendeleev   c. Einstein   d. Molotov

2. Gallium is a solid metal at room temperature, but if you held it in your hand it would _____.

   a. melt   b. explode   c. burn   d. crumble

3. TRUE or FALSE: The physical and chemical properties of gallium were very close to the properties predicted by Mendeleev.

4. According to 1 Corinthians 14:33, "God is not the author of _____." (Fill in the blank.)

5. TRUE or FALSE: All of the elements that Dmitri Mendeleev predicted were eventually discovered.

RESPONSE

"Heavenly Father, Your Word is true. Every promise in it is reliable, and every prophecy will come to pass. You are the Alpha and Omega. You see the end from the beginning. Thank You the blessings of science and the truth of Your Word."

GERMANIUM: "Leeuwenhoek: Father of Microscopy"

"This great and wide sea, in which are innumerable teeming things, living things both small and great" (Ps. 104:25).

DATA

> Germanium is a grayish white metalloid semi-metal. Metalloids have metallic and non-metallic properties.

> Its properties are a cross between the non-metal silicon and the metal tin, which appear above and below germanium in the periodic table.

> It was discovered in 1886 by German chemist Clemens Winkler, who named it for his native country.

> Germanium has two main uses:

1. With metallic and non-metallic properties, germanium is a vital component of semiconductor devices, which make modern computers and electronics possible.

2. Germanium, as GeO_2, is used to make lenses for the best optical microscopes and telescopes.

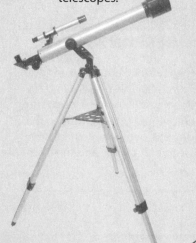

ANALYSIS

Anthoni van Leeuwenhoek (1632–1723) (pronounced "LAY-vun-hook") was born in Holland. He had many jobs in his life. He was trained as a textile merchant and later became a drapery shopkeeper. Later he was a surveyor, a government official, and a wine inspector. But Leeuwenhook is best remembered for something he started doing as a hobby.

In 1668 Anthoni read *Micrographia,* a book by the British scientist Robert Hooke. It contained drawings of images that Hooke had observed through a simple compound microscope: enlarged images of things like insects, leaves, cork, textiles, etc. Hooke used the best microscope available at the time, but it could only magnify images about 20 times. Still, this new way of looking at very small things intrigued the general public, and the book was quite popular.

For Leeuwenhoek, *Micrographia* showed the potential of the magnifying lenses he had used daily to examine fabrics. From a home workshop, he began to make his own microscopes. He developed new ways of grinding lenses and essentially perfected the microscope, as we know it today. Within five years he was able to magnify objects by up to 300 times! Leeuwenhoek was amazed by the new universes he discovered: multitudes of "wee animalcules" (as he called them) in pond and seawater; close-up views of cells in blood, saliva, and even plaque from his teeth; complete life cycles of mollusks, eels, ants, and other insects. He was the first person ever to see bacteria, rotifers, and many other microorganisms.

The scientific world was at first skeptical of Leeuwenhoek's amazing claims; after all, he had no degree or scientific training. Nevertheless, his fame spread and visitors flocked to his little Dutch shop, including the kings of England, Russia, and Prussia. The scientists of his day coveted his microscopes, and he made and sold hundreds of them. He vigorously pursued microscopy, the study of small things, throughout his life. The very week of his death at age 93, he finished a scientific paper for the prestigious Royal Society in London.

BUILDING BETTER LENSES

Germanium, discovered 163 years after Leeuwenhoek's death, also helped to advance the science of microscopy. Leeuwenhoek's lenses were made of ground, polished quartz glass (silicon dioxide or SiO_2). But in recent decades superior microscopes (and telescopes) have been made with germanium dioxide (GeO_2) instead. This new type of glass transmits light with much less distortion, especially in the red side of the spectrum. The periodic table, with germanium lying just below silicon, shows that the oxides of the two elements should be similar, so it is no surprise that either can be used to make glass.

REACTION: *INCOMPREHENSIBLE PERFECTION*

Then God said, "Let the waters abound with an abundance of living creatures . . ." (Gen. 1:20).

So God created great sea creatures and every living thing that moves, with which the waters abounded, according to their kind . . . (Gen. 1:21).

In Leeuwenhoek's time, there was a common belief that insects, worms, and other small animals could appear spontaneously from non-living matter: maggots on exposed meat, worms from mud, insects in wheat, etc. Although we know this to be an unscientific superstition, in the 17th and 18th centuries, most scientists accepted it as fact. They even had a name for this belief: "spontaneous generation."

Leeuwenhoek was well known as a Christian and a Bible believer. He knew from God's Word and his own microscopic studies that living things only come from living things. As the Bible says, animals and plants reproduce "according to their kind." Leeuwenhoek argued against spontaneous generation, and he was the first person ever to observe complete life cycles of ants, fleas, mollusks, and other creatures, to show that no matter how small, all animals have parents. He believed it was sheer folly to think that even the tiny "animalcules" he watched under his lenses could have formed by chance. He once wrote:

"[We] discern most plainly the incomprehensible perfection, the exact order, and the inscrutable providential care with which the most wise Creator and Lord of the Universe had formed in the bodies of these animalcules, which are so small as to escape our sight. . . . And this most wonderful disposition of nature . . . must surely convince all of the absurdity of those old opinions, that living creatures can be produced from corruption of putrefaction."

QUICK QUIZ

1. Like silicon dioxide, germanium dioxide can be used to make glass. Germanium is similar to silicon because it:

    a. appears below silicon in the periodic table.
    b. is an isotope of silicon.
    c. is breakable.
    d. is found in sand.

2. Germanium was discovered by a _____ chemist.

    a. Greek
    b. Swiss
    c. Swedish
    d. German

3. Germanium is used in _____.

    a. coins
    b. computers
    c. food
    d. farming

4. Anthoni van Leeuwenhoek _____.

    a. was trained as a scientist
    b. was a Dutch doctor
    c. invented the modern microscope
    d. was an atheist

5. Leeuwenhoek was the first person to observe bacteria and many other small life forms. He believed that his discoveries disproved the unbiblical idea that life could arise from non-living matter. This false belief was called _____.

RESPONSE

What Leeuwenhoek called an "absurd" theory survived many years after him and well into the time of Charles Darwin, despite the abundance of evidence to the contrary. The idea of spontaneous generation made it easy for people to accept Darwin's theory of evolution. In those days, prior to our knowledge of DNA and the incredible complexity of the cell, it was as easy to believe that simple creatures could evolve into complex ones, as it was to believe that simple creatures evolved from nothing. When many in the scientific world, like Darwin, began to reject a belief in God and the Bible, the theory of evolution became a substitute "creator."

"Lord and Creator of all, help me to be like Anthoni van Leeuwenhoek. Help me to honor You in my work. Show me the unseen things in my life that demonstrate Your providence and wisdom. Amen."

33

As

74.9216

ARSENIC: "And They Shall Drink Poison and Not Die"

"But no man can tame the tongue. It is an unruly evil, full of deadly poison" (James 3:8).

DATA

> Arsenic is a metalloid element, meaning it has some properties of a metal and some of a nonmetal.

> Arsenic exists in three forms: the nonmetallic α- and β-arsenic are yellow and black solids, respectively, while γ-arsenic is dull gray and metallic.

> Various arsenic compounds have been known and used since before the time of Christ. However, credit for its discovery as an element is generally given to Albertus Magnus (1193–1280), a medieval Germanic theologian, scholar, and scientist.

> Despite being a deadly poison in large doses, arsenic is an essential trace element (i.e., at very low concentrations) for many animals and perhaps for humans.

> The term arsenic probably comes from *al-zarnik*, an old Arabic word for a certain arsenic ore.

ANALYSIS

Arsenic has a long reputation as a poison. The ancient Chinese used it to kill rats and insects, and of course people, as did Europeans in the Middle Ages. In medieval Italy and France, there was a black market for arsenic. It was referred to as "succession powder" because it was often used to assassinate kings and dukes to allow a rival to succeed to the throne. It was even used on a pope or two. Others used arsenic to get rid of unwanted spouses or relatives.

In the old days, if you wanted to get away with murder, arsenic was the ideal poison! It could be given in small doses over a period of weeks. Initial symptoms were weakness, vomiting, and diarrhea. As the poison accumulated in the body, the effects would worsen, with heart failure as the eventual cause of death. Because the symptoms were so general and similar to several diseases, it was hard to prove poisoning, and there was no test to detect the small amount of arsenic needed to kill. That was the situation until 1836, when a British physician named James Marsh developed a very sensitive test to prove cases of arsenic poisoning.

Despite its toxicity, arsenic has beneficial applications. Its compounds have uses in the treatment of sleeping sickness and leukemia, though it is now used mostly in veterinary medicine. Prior to the discovery of penicillin, a form of arsenic was the preferred treatment for syphilis. Until recently, arsenic was used to pressure-treat lumber for outdoor use. (The arsenic kept termites and fungus from attacking the wood. Now copper is used instead.) Finally, the crystalline compound, gallium arsenide, is becoming increasingly useful to make powerful lasers.

POISONS IN THE BIBLE

Arsenic is not mentioned in the Bible, but several other poisons are:

- *Hosea 10:4 says judgment against oath breakers "springs up like hemlock in the furrows of the field."*

- *Job compares his suffering to poisoned arrows from the Almighty, in Job 6:4.*

- *The venom of snakes and scorpions is mentioned in several places in the Bible: Deuteronomy 32:24, 33; Ezekiel 2:6; Luke 11:12; etc.*

In Luke 10:19 Jesus told a group of 70 of His disciples, whom He had sent out to spread the gospel, that they would be given "authority to trample on serpents and scorpions, and over all the power of the enemy, and nothing shall by any means hurt you."

Later He made an even broader promise regarding His followers: "And these signs will follow those who believe: In My name they will cast out demons; they will speak with new tongues; they will take up serpents; and if they drink anything deadly, it will by no means hurt them . . ." (Mark 16:17–18).

REACTION: *IT WILL BY NO MEANS HURT THEM*

"In my name . . . they will take up serpents; and if they drink anything deadly, it will by no means hurt them" (Mark 16:17–18).

This is a very controversial statement in the Bible, but it doesn't need to be.

Some people say that Jesus only meant the verse figuratively. After all, Christians are just as vulnerable to poisons and venom as anyone else. But then what about the apostle Paul's experience on Malta (Acts 28:1–11)?

A snake bit Paul when he was gathering wood for a fire. Up to 300 of the islanders on Malta witnessed the event and they knew the snake to be deadly. When they saw how it dangled from Paul's hand until he shook it off, the Maltans were sure he would die. But Paul was under God's protection, so the venom had no effect. Surely, this was in fulfillment of Christ's promise in Mark 16:18. Paul and Luke stayed on Malta for three months before continuing to Rome, and many of the Maltans were persuaded by their preaching and Paul's miraculous resistance to the snake.

In many Third World countries, deliberate poisoning is a real threat to missionaries and newly converted Christians. For example, in Haiti, voodoo priests are knowledgeable about poisons and venomous snakes. They see Christian missionaries as a threat. These priests have been known to use their powerful poisons against the missionaries. In such places, missionaries rely on Jesus' promise in Mark 16 for their protection and the safety of their families and converts.

This is not the same as the dangerous custom of "snake handling" that is practiced in some areas of the southern United States. Remember that the promise of God's protection in Mark 16:18 is set in the context of the Great Commission: "Go into all the world and preach the gospel to every creature" (Mark 16:15). Deliberate "snake handling" or drinking of poison does not glorify God or spread the gospel.

QUICK QUIZ

1. Arsenic is categorized as which of the following?

   a. a metalloid   b. a metal   c. a non-metal   d. a transition metal

2. TRUE or FALSE: Arsenic is a poison in large doses, but in very small amounts it may be vital for human life and health.

3. TRUE or FALSE: In the Middle Ages, arsenic was often used to assassinate people in positions of power.

4. Until recent years, lumber for outdoor use was treated with arsenic to resist against _____.

   a. insects   b. fire   c. rain   d. kids

5. The physician who developed first medical test to detect arsenic poisoning was named _____ (Fill in the blank.)

RESPONSE

"Heavenly Father, thank You for Your promise of protection. Like David, I rely on You for defense from my enemies and from the poisonous influences of this sinful world. Surround me with Your love and grace. Amen."

34
Se
78.96

SELENIUM: "The Moon Goddess"

"But in those days, after that tribulation, the sun shall be darkened, and the moon [Greek: selene] shall not give her light"(Mark 13:24).

DATA

> Selenium is a soft metalloid that exists in three different forms: a gray metallic form, a reddish powder, or a black crystal. Like other metalloids, it has metallic and non-metallic properties.

> Chemically, selenium behaves like a cross between the non-metal sulfur and the metal tellurium, which appear above and below selenium in the periodic table.

> Discovered in 1817 by the great Swedish chemist Jons Jacob Berzelius. He named it after the Greek goddess of the moon, Selene (also called Diana.)

> Selenium is a rare element but it has industrial applications, based on its highly unusual light sensitive behavior. (When placed in darkness, selenium does not conduct electricity, but in bright sunlight, it is an excellent conductor. It also converts sunlight into electricity.)

> Selenium is important in trace amounts for good health.

ANALYSIS

We may speak of the "man in the moon," but throughout history the moon has been thought of as female. In the verse above, quoted from the King James Version, even Jesus refers to the moon as "her." (Most modern translations use "its" instead of "her," but the female pronoun accurately reflects Greek usage of the time.)

Selene is the Greek word for "moon," and it was also the name of the moon goddess of the Greeks. She was the sister of Helios, the sun god (see Element No. 2). The Greeks had other names for her — Artemis or Cynthia — but in the Bible she is referred to by yet another of her names — Diana. The story of Paul's conflict with the worshipers of Diana in the city of Ephesus appears in Acts 19 and 20.

"Great is Diana of the Ephesians!" (Acts 19:34). This could be considered the "motto" of the city of Ephesus. Their fabulous Temple of Diana was one of the Seven Wonders of the World. Worshipers came from all over Greek civilization to worship Diana there. (The temple's massive ruins remain a tourist attraction to this day.) Ephesus was a regional capital and a rich port city. The silversmiths of Ephesus had a powerful trade union, and they made quite a bit of money by making and selling statues of the goddess for use as idols.

This pagan city was one of the places where Paul went on his third missionary journey to establish a church. Paul faced much resistance there, both from the Jews and the Greeks, but still the church grew. Soon, so many Ephesians were getting saved that it began to affect the sale of idols of Diana. The silversmiths, seeing their business suffer, rioted and dragged some of Paul's followers to the center of town. Fortunately, the town leaders knew that Paul was a Roman citizen, and they quieted the crowd for fear that the Roman army (who controlled Greece at that time) would come into the city to stop the riot by force.

After at least three years of ministry in Ephesus, Paul left to start other churches, but Ephesus always held a special place in his heart.

REACTION: *THE CHURCH OF EPHESUS*

Paul, an apostle of Jesus Christ by the will of God, to the saints who are in Ephesus, and faithful in Christ Jesus: Grace to you and peace from God our Father and the Lord Jesus Christ" (Eph. 1:1–2).

Of all the churches that Paul started, the Ephesian church was unique. He spent more time there than at any of the other churches he founded. The church grew and was strong and did many good works. It is no wonder that when Paul said his final good-byes to them before leaving for Jerusalem, "They all wept freely, and fell on Paul's neck and kissed him, sorrowing most of all for the words which he spoke, that they would see his face no more" (Acts 20:37–38). Later on, Paul sent Timothy there to become its pastor (1 Tim. 1:3). According to early church writings, the apostle John was their pastor in his later years, and it was in Ephesus that John wrote his five New Testament books.

Later, when Paul was held in a Roman prison, his thoughts returned to his friends at Ephesus, and from prison he wrote them a letter that we have come to know as the Book of Ephesians. This book is considered one of the grandest and most profound books of the Bible. Some of the doctrines it sets forth are the believer's standing in Christ and the spiritual unity of Jewish and Gentile Christians. It also gives practical advice to Christians to live a Spirit-filled life.

Because of Paul's faithfulness in taking the gospel of Christ into a hostile, pagan city, a great church was founded, and we have Paul's Letter to the Ephesians to guide us in our spiritual walks today.

(The church of Ephesus is mentioned three times in Scripture: in Acts 19 and 20, in Paul's Epistle to the Ephesians, and finally as one of the "Seven Churches of Asia" referred to in Revelation chapters 2 and 3.)

QUICK QUIZ

1. The Greek word for "moon" is _____.

    a. helios   b. selene   c. ephesus   d. berzelius

2. Chemically, selenium is said to be a cross between _____ and tellurium.

    a. iron   b. hydrogen   c. lead   d. sulfur

3. When exposed to sunlight, the _____ of selenium increases.

    a. electrical conduction   b. heat conduction   c. density   d. hardness

4. Ephesus was the site of the ancient Greek temple of _____.

    a. Zeus   b. Neptune   c. Diana   d. Athens

5. In addition to the Books of Acts and Ephesians, Ephesus is referred to in the Book of _____.

    a. Matthew   b. Romans   c. Hebrews   d. Revelation

RESPONSE

"Lord, I thank You for Paul's faithfulness. Help me to be faithful and brave and to go where You would send me in my spiritual walk." Amen.

35	
Br	
79.904	

BROMINE: "The 'Smelly' Gas"

"For what purpose to Me comes frankincense from Sheba, and sweet cane from a far country? Your burnt offerings are not acceptable, nor your sacrifices sweet to Me" (Jer. 6:20).

DATA

> Bromine is the third member of the halogen family of elements (Group 17).

> Like the other halogens, plus oxygen, nitrogen, and hydrogen, bromine exists as diatomic molecules with the formula Br_2.

> It is a dark-red liquid at room temperature, but its vapor irritates the eyes, nose, and throat.

> Bromine has a foul—smelling odor, somewhat like chlorine.

> The French scientist Antoine-Jerome Balard discovered it in 1826, deriving it from seawater.

> Bromine comes from *bromos,* a Greek word meaning "odor," due to bromine's foul smell.

> Chemicals called "bromides" were once used a sedatives for humans, and are still used by vets.

ANALYSIS

Many elements in the periodic table derive their names from the colors of their compounds, but only two get their names due to their smells. Bromine comes from a Greek word, *bromos,* meaning "stench" or "foul smell," due to its bad smell. Osmium (number 76) is known for its unpleasant-smelling compounds; its name is from a different Greek word, *osmos,* which means "odor."

SENSE OF SMELL

The sense of smell has always been an important part of chemical identification. Before there were more sophisticated tools for chemical analysis, chemists developed tables of odors and tastes to classify chemicals. Compounds of sulfur, ammonia, and even cyanide (!) were identified by their smells. The large class of organic chemicals called "aromatics" (benzene, toluene, etc.) is so named because of the sweet "aroma" that many of them have.

Of course, this method of "analysis by odor" had a major drawback: it could be deadly! Many odorous compounds are strong poisons. Some arsenic compounds were identified by their "nauseating odors." The chemical hydrogen cyanide (HCN) has a telltale odor of "bitter almonds." For some chemists, bitter almond was the last odor they would ever smell.

The famous scientist Sir Humphry Davy was fascinated by gaseous compounds of nitrogen and oxygen, many of which are dangerous. But with limited means of analysis, he often resorted to his sense of smell. Davy nearly died from inhalation of the sweet-smelling gas nitrous oxide (or "laughing gas") and had breathing problems late in life due to lung damage.

SENSE OF TASTE

You may wonder why so many dictionaries refer to the taste and odor of elements and compounds. For example, oxygen is defined as a "colorless, odorless, tasteless gas." Who, you might ask, goes around tasting gasses? That phraseology goes back to the early days of chemistry when chemists classified chemicals by their tastes. Acids were identified as sour-tasting and bases were identified as bitter.

Some chemicals are harmless to ingest but many definitely are not. As an example, early chemists described lead compounds as "sweet-tasting." Until about a hundred years ago, wine makers would drop a tiny lead pellet in every bottle of wine. As the wine aged and the pellet dissolved, it gave the wine a sweet taste. More recently, lead-based house paint has been a major health threat to young children who sometimes lick or eat the flaking paint for its sugary taste.

Finally, the element we know as beryllium was originally called "glucinium" meaning the "sweet metal." Its discoverer, Louis Nicolas Vauquelin, named it that because initially the only way he could tell the difference between aluminum and "glucinium" was by the taste of their compounds. (Beryllium compounds are sweet; aluminum compounds are tasteless.) Eventually, "glucinium" was dropped in favor of beryllium, due to the element's association with the gem beryl.

REACTION: *THERE IS A STENCH*

Jesus said, "Take away the stone." Martha, the sister of him who was dead, said to Him, "Lord, by this time there is a stench, for he has been dead four days" (John 11:39). [The Greek word for stench here is *ozo,* where we get the English word "ozone" (from its smell).]

The raising of Lazarus from the dead is the greatest miracle performed by Jesus in His earthly ministry (other than His own resurrection, of course). It clearly demonstrates Jesus' mastery over nature and even life and death. It also shows His mastery over chemistry. (The story of Lazarus appears in chapter 11 of John.)

One day Jesus got an urgent message from His friends Mary and Martha. Their brother, Lazarus, was deathly ill. They had seen Jesus heal others and they begged Him to come and save their brother. By the time Jesus received the message, He knew that Lazarus had already died and He told His disciples so.

Lazarus and his sisters lived in Bethany, a town near Jerusalem. But Jesus was on the other side of the Jordan River. When Jesus finally arrived in Bethany, it was a sad scene indeed. Lazarus had been dead for four days and he had been placed in a tomb. Many neighbors had come to comfort the grieving sisters and all were weeping. Even Jesus was touched; He "groaned in His spirit" and wept as well.

HE STINKETH

When Jesus first arrived at his friends' house and wanted to go to the tomb, Martha was reluctant. After four days, she knew that Lazarus's corpse was already decaying. She said, "There is a stench." (The King James Version puts it more bluntly: "He stinketh.")

When a body decays it generates a variety of odorous vapors. One of the main sources is protein, due to its sulfur content. Proteins break down into very smelly gasses like hydrogen sulfide (H_2S) and mercaptan (CH_3SH). As decay continues, more complex molecules with names like cadaverine and putrine are generated, each with their own unpleasant smells.

Jesus went to the tomb and called out loudly: "Lazarus, come forth!" Then, to the amazement of all, Lazarus appeared at the door of the tomb. He looked like a mummy. Lazarus was all bound up in strips of grave-cloth and people had to unwrap him. The Bible says because of this miracle, many came to believe in Jesus.

Just as He made blood flow in Lazarus's veins and put breath in his lungs again, Jesus also reversed the decay process, so that the smell of death was gone.

QUICK QUIZ

1. Bromine comes from the Greek word *bromos* which means _____.

   a. brown   b. smelly   c. heavy   d. burning

2. Bromine was originally found in _____.

   a. seawater   b. the atmosphere   c. plants   d. iron ore

3. Bromine is an example of a (an) _____.

   a. noble gas   b. alkali   c. halogen   d. metalloid

4. Bromine molecules are _____.

   a. organic   b. inert   c. diatomic   d. all of the above

5. _____ was the brother of Mary and Martha. (Fill in the blank.)

RESPONSE

After their brother was raised up, Mary and Martha made a supper for Lazarus and Jesus and His disciples. It was here that Mary found a special way to express her appreciation for Jesus, one that also involved the sense of smell. "Then Mary took a pound of very costly oil of spikenard, anointed the feet of Jesus, and wiped His feet with her hair. And the house was filled with the fragrance of the oil" (John 12:3).

"Lord, help me to live a life that is pleasing to You in every way. Just as Lazarus was raised up, I know I will be raised someday as well, whether it be from the grave or by the rapture. Help me to be faithful until that day comes. In the name of Jesus, who raises the dead. Amen."

36
Kr
83.798

KRYPTON: "The Hidden Gas"

"[The Lord will] bring to light the hidden things [Greek: krypton] of darkness, and reveal the counsels of the hearts. Then each one's praise will come from God" (1 Cor. 4:5).

DATA

> Krypton is from the Greek word *kryptos,* meaning "hidden" or "mysterious."

> Krypton is a colorless, odorless, and dense gas.

> It was discovered by Sir William Ramsey and Morris Travers in 1898.

> Krypton is one of the noble gasses, sometimes called the inert gasses.

ANALYSIS

Toward the end of the 19th century, scientists had begun to believe that most major discoveries had already been made. The whole world had largely been explored and mapped. The physical laws of gravity and thermodynamics were well developed. The stars had all been charted (or so they thought) and the motions of the planets were well understood. Darwin's theory was thought to explain the origin of all the species. Many scientists were beginning to think that anything worth discovering had already been found.

As further examples of this belief, consider the following: (1) It was believed the atmosphere had been thoroughly investigated. Air was made up of oxygen and nitrogen in a fixed ratio with variable amounts of carbon dioxide and water vapor. (2) The periodic table itself was considered to be structurally complete. Certainly, there were elements to be discovered, but they would be found and inserted neatly into the remaining spaces in Mendeleev's periodic table.

But as usual, just when scientists begin to get complacent, thinking they know everything, someone comes along to shake things up. In this case, the shake-up came from a Scottish chemist named William Ramsey (1852–1916). Ramsey was about to uncover a whole new "hidden" column in the periodic table.

In 1894 William Ramsey and his partner, Lord Rayleigh, startled the scientific world when they announced his discovery of a new gaseous element, which they called argon. (See Argon, Element 18.) This non-reactive, inert gas had gone unnoticed throughout the whole history of chemistry. All the great minds of science had gone about their discovering and inventing, totally oblivious to this inert gas inhabiting the very air that they breathed. A hidden gas!

Of course Ramsey knew of Mendeleev's periodic table, now 25 years old. He knew that all of the other elements existed in columns of similar elements with different molecular weights. So he became convinced that there were other hidden gasses, similar to argon, waiting to be found.

Just a year later, Ramsey detected a gas that was given off by a radioactive, uranium ore. He collected it and determined that it was yet another hidden gas, lighter than argon but just as inert: helium.

In 1898 Ramsey tried out a new method to find additional inert gasses. This time he had another partner, Morris Travers. They used super-cooled liquid air to separate out various components of the atmosphere based on their boiling points. In the same year, Ramsey and Travers discovered three more inert gases. In order, they were krypton (the "hidden" gas), neon (the "new" gas), and xenon (the "strange" gas).

Sir William Ramsey holds a unique place in the history of science. No other person has discovered an entire unknown column of the periodic table. His discoveries, with his co-workers, led to many technical advances and a fuller understanding of the nature of atoms and elements. As Rayleigh, the co-discoverer of argon, put it, they "sought out . . . the [hidden] works of the Lord" (referring to Ps. 111:2).

REACTION: *THE HIDDEN WORKS OF THE LORD*

The works of the LORD are great, sought out of all them that have pleasure therein (Ps. 111:2).

Currently, in many so-called institutions of higher learning it can be "dangerous" to be a Christian. Scientific creationism is scoffed at and creationists are discriminated against. Even if an agnostic scientist, after being awed and overwhelmed by the incredible complexity of life and universe, dares to consider the possible involvement of an intelligent force, he is likely to be ridiculed and denied tenure and degrees. Some have even lost their jobs. Almost every major scientific body has taken firm stands against Creation and Intelligent Design. This has not always been the case.

In 1904 William Ramsey and Lord Rayleigh each received Nobel Prizes for their joint discovery of the noble gas, argon. They were life-long friends and both were well known as devout Christians. They believed that in their study of science they were merely uncovering the hidden things of God.

Lord Rayleigh published a five-volume collection of his works late in his life. His life's motto was printed in the front of each volume. Taken from Psalm 111:2, it read: "The works of the Lord are great, sought out of all them that have pleasure therein." For these men, there was pleasure in seeking out God's works.

William Ramsey was an especially remarkable man. He was known as a great linguist. He sometimes amazed international audiences of scientists by giving a single lecture using four languages — English, German, French, and Italian, all of which he spoke perfectly. As a youngster he attended church in Glasgow, and it was during its long Calvinist sermons that he developed a technique for learning new languages. He knew the Bible in English so well he hardly needed to read it, so he always took a French or German Bible to church to follow the sermons. Ramsey also worked on ideas in geometry by studying the church's stained glass windows.

Rayleigh and Ramsey demonstrate that biblical faith and scientific excellence can and should go hand in hand.

1. The first noble gas discovered by William Ramsey was _____. (Fill in the blank.)

2. Ramsey's discovery led to a new _____ in the periodic table.

   a. column   b. row   c. period   d. level

3. Helium is given off by _____.

   a. carbon   b. hydrogen   c. oxygen   d. uranium

4. Krypton comes from the Greek word *kryptos* which means _____.

   a. lazy   b. strange   c. hidden   d. planet

5. In 1904 William Ramsey and Lord Rayleigh received what award for the discovery of argon?

RESPONSE

"Lord, thank You for the blessed opportunity to seek out Your hidden works. Help me to never be ashamed to be known as a Christian. Amen."

37

Rb

85.4678

RUBIDIUM: "Just How Old Is That Rock?"

"Thy word is true from the beginning" (Ps. 119:160).

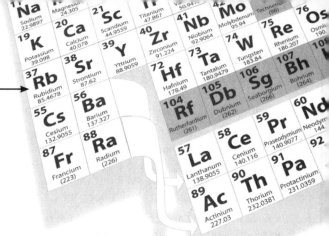

ANALYSIS

How old is planet earth? Is the earth 4.5 billion years old as evolutionists claim? Or are creationists right to say the world was created less than 10,000 years ago? Ever since Darwin, scientists on both sides have used arguments from every field of science to try to prove their views. Biology, astronomy, paleontology, geology, and physics: each of these areas of study has something to say on the issue. The discovery of radioactivity in 1896 would eventually lead to the development of new tools to answer the question. And rubidium and strontium would be two of the key elements employed.

ISOTOPES. Natural rubidium exists as two separate isotopes: rubidium-85 (with 37 protons and 48 neutrons) and rubidium-87 (37 protons, 50 neutrons). Rb-85 is stable, but Rb-87, with two extra neutrons in its nucleus, is unstable. This means that Rb-87 atoms spontaneously decay or break apart at a specific rate. In other words, rubidium-87 is a radioactive isotope. Rb-85 is not.

If a rock contains rubidium, over time some of its Rb-87 atoms will turn into atoms of strontium-87 (a stable isotope of strontium with 38 protons and 49 neutrons). Rubidium-87 has a long half-life (about 50 billion years) and this makes the so-called rubidium-strontium method a very popular, and supposedly reliable, radioactive dating technique.

When a volcano erupts, the lava cools to form rocks, which contain small amounts of Rb-87 and Sr-87. Rocks formed by ancient volcanoes should contain less Rb-87 and more Sr-87 than more recent rocks. Seemingly, analyzing the amounts of each isotope in a rock will tell you its age. So a really old lava rock should prove that the earth is really old as well.

THE GRAND CANYON TEST

The Grand Canyon in Arizona has experienced volcanic activity throughout its history. For example, volcanic rock in the bottom layers of the canyon had to be there before the canyon was formed. However, a volcano along the rim of the western Grand Canyon erupted 1,000 to 3,000 years ago, sending cascades of lava all the way down the side of the canyon into the Colorado River below.

Recently, samples of both the "ancient" and "recent" volcanic rocks were analyzed by the rubidium-strontium method, as described above. The ancient rocks from the canyon bottom were determined to be 1.07 billion years old, apparently proving that the earth is much older than 10,000 years. However, the rocks formed by the recent volcanic activity tested to be even older: 1.34 billion years. This is not possible, of course.

This is an example of the failure of radioactive methods to properly determine the age of the earth. In the case of the Grand Canyon rocks, the error is probably due to wrong assumptions about the initial concentration of isotopes in the lava that formed the rocks. Evolutionists say that the rubidium-strontium method should not be used on recent lava flows, because they typically give wrong results. This only begs the question: how can we trust dates for older volcanic rocks? (For further reading, see *Grand Canyon: Monument to Catastrophe,* Austin, Steven (Editor), Institute for Creation Research, 1994; or www.icr.org/article/353.)

DATA

> Rubidium was discovered by Robert Bunsen (inventor of the Bunsen burner) and Gustav Kirchhoff in 1861. They first identified it by spectroscopic analysis.

> Rubidium is a very soft, silvery white metal. It has a very low melting point. (39°C/102°F).

> Rubidium spontaneously combusts when exposed to air.

> Its name is from the Latin *rubidus,* meaning "deep red," from the ruby-red color it produces under spectroscopic analysis.

> Natural rubidium exists as two isotopes: one stable and one radioactive.

REACTION: *IN THE BEGINNING*

In the beginning God created the heavens and the earth (Gen. 1:1).

In addition to the rubidium-strontium method, there are other combinations of elements used to play the "radioactive dating game": potassium-argon, uranium-lead, and, of course, carbon-14. All of them are based on measuring and comparing the concentrations of "mother" and "daughter" isotopes. All of them require multiple assumptions to be made about contamination, initial compositions, and the migration of atoms into and out of the sample analyzed.

Often the first step is to make an assumption about the supposed age of the sample. Based on such assumptions, the "best" radioactive method is chosen that will give the "most accurate" results. You can see why creationists are dubious about these assumptions.

The study of radioactive processes can provide powerful evidence of creation. Dr. Robert Gentry, formerly of Oak Ridge National Laboratory, has spent much of his life in the study of "polonium halos": microscopic spheres found in rocks all over the world. These halos provide powerful, un-refuted evidence that the earth had to be created almost instantaneously. This evidence will be examined in the entry for Polonium, Element 82.

QUICK QUIZ

1. Robert Bunsen was the co-discoverer of rubidium and the inventor of what laboratory device?

2. Radioactive atoms of rubidium break down to form what element?

    a. strontium   b. uranium   c. thorium   d. tin

3. Rubidium-85 has 37 protons and 48 _____.

    a. neutrons   b. electrons   c. isotopes   d. orbitals

4. Several layers of rock in the _____ _____ are volcanic in origin. (Fill in the blanks.)

5. TRUE or FALSE: Natural samples of rubidium ore invariably contain radioactive and non-radioactive atoms.

RESPONSE

"Lord of all creation, I thank You for Your Word that tells the true history of the world. It is the source of wisdom and salvation. I praise Your name. Amen."

38	
Sr	
87.62	

STRONTIUM: "Sir Humphry Davy: The Faith of a Scientist"

"I have fought the good fight, I have finished the race, I have kept the faith" (2 Timothy 4:7).

DATA

> In 1790 the Irishman Dr. Adair Crawford reported the detection of a new element in a mineral called strontia. The element became known as strontium.

> In 1808 Sir Humphry Davy isolated strontium from strontia using the method he had previously used to isolate other elements.

> Strontia was first found in a lead mine in the town of Strontian, Scotland.

> Strontium (pronounced stron'-tee-um) is a soft, silvery metal.

> Strontium compounds are often used to make the bright red colors of fireworks displays.

ANALYSIS

In 1800 the Italian physicist Count Alessandro Volta (1745–1827) created the first battery when he stacked alternating zinc and silver discs, separated by cardboard discs soaked in saltwater. (Because of the way the discs were stacked, this type of battery became known as the "voltaic pile.") He found that when he attached wires to the top and bottom discs he could generate an electric current. Volta's batteries could be made extremely powerful by adding more plates or connecting several batteries in series. (The electrical term "volt" is named after Count Volta.) Volta discovered that when he ran wires from his batteries into a container of water, the electric current traveling through the water would actually break apart the molecules (H_2O) to make pure oxygen (O_2) at the negatively charged wire and pure hydrogen (H_2) at the other positive wire. This process of generating hydrogen and oxygen became known as electrolysis.

When the English scientist Sir Humphry Davy learned of the Italian's discovery, he was intrigued. If electricity could be used to decompose water into elements, he believed surely other compounds could be broken down in this way, too. At this time Davy was already a very successful scientist. He had attained a prestigious position (professor of chemistry) at the Royal Institution, an organization devoted to using the advances of science to benefit the poor. Davy used his position there to amass a great collection of Volta-inspired batteries.

A chemical called "potash" (which we now know as potassium carbonate) was commonly used in laboratories at the time, and this was the first substance Davy tried to decompose by electrolysis. First he dissolved the potash in water and applied the electric current. This was a failure; the only thing he generated was oxygen and hydrogen — just like water with no potash.

Davy didn't give up. He tried several different ways of applying a current to potash. Each time he was disappointed until he finally tried heating the dry potash above its melting point (891°C/1636°F) and applying the current to it in its molten form. He was thrilled when he found little balls of a silvery metal forming at one of the electrodes. These globules were pure potassium metal, and Davy was the first person ever to see potassium in this form. Since Davy found this new metal in potash, he named it "potassium."

In the years that followed, Davy discovered many new elements by this technique, including sodium, magnesium, boron, calcium, and barium.

In 1908 Davy was investigating an interesting mineral called strontia, which came from a mine near Strontian, Scotland. He soon was able to produce yet another new metallic element. He named it strontium, after the mineral.

The isolation of strontium metal was just one of Sir Humphry Davy's many contributions to science and to life in the 19th century.

REACTION: *THE GOOD FIGHT*

Sir Humphry Davy was a truly amazing man. He was very famous in his time — as famous as a rock star or a movie star today. His brilliant lectures, complete with flashy chemistry demonstrations, were attended by throngs of admirers, kings and queens, and common people from all over Europe. Some of his best friends were the poet Samuel Taylor Coleridge and Dr. Peter Roget, who created the thesaurus. Davy wrote a classic manual on angling that fishermen still refer to.

Davy was so highly respected on both sides of the English Channel that Napoleon himself awarded him a prestigious science medal. (Even though England and France were at war at the time!)

Davy's discovery of so many elements and his invention of the mine safety lamp were just a few of Davy's scientific accomplishments. He discovered the anesthetic properties of nitrous oxide (N_2O or laughing gas) and suggested its use in surgery. (Of course, it is still used in dentistry to this day!) Davy considered his young apprentice, Michael Faraday, to be his "greatest discovery." Faraday went on to have as great an influence on science as Davy, but in a different field: electricity.

QUICK QUIZ

1. Strontium creates _____ colors in fireworks.

   a. yellow   b. green   c. blue   d. red

2. What Italian scientist invented the first modern battery?

3. Sir Humphry Davy first isolated which of the following elements?

   a. sodium   b. strontium   c. potassium   d. all of the above

4. The use of an electric current to decompose a chemical compound is called_____. (Fill in the blank.)

5. Humphry Davy believed that the _____ is the result of God's power and wisdom.

   a. periodic table   b. natural world   c. voltaic pile   d. theory of evolution

RESPONSE

Despite his fame, brilliance, and wealth, Humphry Davy remained a devout Christian who always glorified God in his work. Toward the end of his life, Davy journeyed through Europe. He especially longed to see Rome, the city so important in Christian history. It was there that he wrote his last book, which contained many acknowledgments of his faith, such as the following:

". . . being sure from revelation that God is omnipotent and omnipresent, it appears to me no improper use of our facilities to trace even in the natural universe the acts of His power and the results of His wisdom, and to draw parallels from the finite to the infinite mind. Remember, we are taught that man was created in the image of God" (From Davy's book, *Consolations in Travel*, 1829).

Davy passed away in Switzerland late in his travels with his wife and some close friends by his side. Like the apostle Paul, he could claim:

"I have fought the good fight, I have finished the race, I have kept the faith. Finally, there is laid up for me the crown of righteousness, which the Lord, the righteous judge, will give to me on that Day" (2 Tim. 4: 7–8).

"Heavenly Father, thank You for men and women of principle who honor You and Your Word in all their endeavors. Help me to be like them. Grant me opportunities to help others today. Help me to recognize these opportunities when they come and to act on them. Amen."

39	
Y	
88.9059	

YTTRIUM: "The Key to Television"

"I will set nothing wicked before my eyes; I hate the work of those who fall away; it shall not cling to me" (Ps. 101:3).

DATA

> Yttrium is a silvery, ductile metal. It is soft, lightweight, and fairly reactive.

> Yttrium was discovered by the Finnish chemist Johan Gadolin in 1794.

> Its name is from the mineral called yttria, which in turn was named after the Swedish town Ytterby where it was found.

> Yttrium oxysulfide is the chemical that provides the red color of color television screens. Therefore, yttrium makes color television possible.

ANALYSIS

Television was first developed in the early 1920s. It was made possible due to the invention of the cathode ray tube or CRT. A CRT is a large glass tube with a cathode or electron generator in the back. The cathode creates a stream of electrons that travel in a straight line and strike the front part of the tube, also called the screen. However, since electrons are negatively charged, the electron stream can be deflected with electromagnetic coils inside the CRT. In this way, the stream of electrons can be controlled to strike the screen in certain places and produce images.

The inside of the screen of the CRT is coated with chemical compounds (mostly metal oxides and metal sulfides) called phosphors. These phosphor compounds are usually poor electrical conductors. This means that when the electron beam strikes the phosphor-coated tube, the phosphors absorb (rather than conduct) the electrons' energy. The absorbed electrical energy is re-emitted as light energy. The frequency (or color) of the light generated depends on the phosphor used on the CRT screen. [NOTE: You should not confuse the term phosphor with the element phosphorus. "Phosphor" and "phosphorus" each come from the same Greek word, but otherwise there is no connection.]

COLOR TELEVISION

Television developers knew that creating a color television would require the development of phosphors for three colors of light: red, blue, and green. All the colors of the rainbow and every blend of color in between can be made from these three. After years of research, they were able to find many types of suitable blue and green phosphors. But the red phosphors they had found gave off only a faint red light. So early color TVs had a really faint picture screen because the blues and greens were kept dim so they would not overpower the faint red phosphors. Early color TV sets were not a success.

But research into new phosphor materials eventually paid off. Most modern color televisions use phosphors made of yttrium oxysulfide (Y_2O_2S) to produce a very bright and long-lasting red color. Without yttrium, color television as we know it would not exist.

REACTION: *PROFANE AND IDLE BABBLINGS*

O Timothy! Guard what was committed to your trust, avoiding the profane and idle babblings and contradictions of what is falsely called knowledge — by professing it some have strayed concerning the faith. Grace be with you. Amen (1 Tim. 6:20–21).

The invention of television is one of the marvels of the modern life. It has truly changed the world in many ways. It dominates the lives of many and affects all of us whether we watch it or not. The same technology makes the computer and the Internet possible.

Every form of technology can be used for good or bad. Weapons can provide food for one's family and protection from threats, but they are also used to murder and steal. The first book published on the printing press was the Bible, but soon it was utilized for many other forms, from anti-Christian literature to pornography. Television is no different.

> Does your television add to your life or is it a thief that takes away time you should spend with God or your family? Does it take away your physical fitness as you sit idly before it?

> Does it help you in your Christian walk or is it a tempter that draws you away from holiness?

> Is your television a blessing or a curse?

PROFANE AND IDLE BABBLINGS

Timothy was the son of a Greek father and a devout Jewish mother (Acts 16:1). He was raised as a Greek, but his mother taught him in accordance with the Scriptures. After hearing Paul preach, Timothy, his mother, and his grandmother all gave their hearts to Christ (2 Tim. 1:5). Timothy grew in this faith and joined Paul in his missions work. Eventually, Paul chose Timothy to succeed him as pastor of the large, influential church of Ephesus. First and Second Timothy were letters written by Paul to instruct Timothy in how to carry out his duties.

Paul was well educated in Greek philosophy. The things that Paul warned Timothy against in the verse above ("profane and idle babblings," etc.) probably represented Paul's view of Greek culture. Greece was a prosperous nation with many gods and goddesses but without knowledge of the true God. The Greeks looked at philosophers, poets, and playwrights as the enlightened of their age. In many ways, Greek culture resembled many aspects of our entertainment-centered lifestyles, especially television.

Paul's words to Timothy still have a lot of meaning for us today.

QUICK QUIZ

1. A yttrium compound produces the _____ color of a color television screen.

   a. red   b. yellow   c. blue   d. green

2. A television screen is also called a _____ ray tube or CRT.

   a. calcium   b. cathode   c. copper   d. conduction

3. The electron beam in a television screen is controlled by an electro- _____. (Fill in the blank.)

4. The tiny dots on a TV screen are called _____.

   a. phosphors   b. sulfurs   c. catheters   d. uranium

5. Watching too much television can _____.

   a. expose us to unholy   b. encourage a sedentary   c. take away time we should   d. all of the above
      entertainment   lifestyle   be spending with God

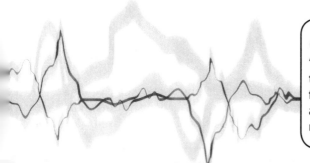

RESPONSE

"Heavenly Father, help me to limit the negative influence of television and the corrupt culture of our time in my life. Let me feed my soul only with ideas and images that truly honor You and advance my growth as a Christian. In Christ's holy and righteous name. Amen."

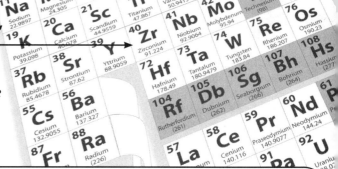

40
Zr
91.224

ZIRCONIUM: "Zircon: Foundation Stone"

"The foundations of the wall of the city were adorned with all kinds of precious stones" (Rev. 21:19). (Zircon [or jacinth] is the 11th of the 12 foundation stones of the heavenly city listed in Revelation.)

DATA

> Zirconium is a grayis white, lustrous, corrosion-resistant metal.

> It is often used in electronics and the nuclear power industry, due to the metal's toughness.

> The German Martin Klaproth identified and named zirconium as an element in 1789. Jons Jacob Berzelius of Sweden isolated it in 1824.

> Zirconium gets its name from the mineral/gemstone "zircon." (Zircon comes from the Persian word *zargun* meaning "gold-like.")

> Impure zircon (the mineral called zirconia) is used in ceramics and other industries, but most people are familiar with its pure form as a beautiful, diamond-like gemstone. (The formula for zircon is $ZrSiO_4$.)

> In the Bible, zircon is known as "jacinth" or "hyacinth." It was one of the 12 gems in the priest's breastplate (Exod. 28) and one of the 12 foundation stones mentioned in Revelation 21.

ANALYSIS

Rabanus Maurus (780–856 A.D.) was a priest in the time of Charlemagne. He was known as a great scholar and theologian. Among his many writings were commentaries on 33 books of the Bible and books about practical and doctrinal issues. In 847 Maurus became the archbishop of Mainz, Germany, his hometown. Maurus died in 856, but his memory is still celebrated in the German cities where he lived and taught.

Between 814 and 817, he made a pilgrimage to the Holy Land. This may have been when Maurus became intrigued by the gemstones of Israel. He studied the 12 foundation stones of the heavenly city in Revelation 21 and wrote a description of what he believed each stone represented in the life of a Christian:

1.) Maurus said that jasper represents "the truth of faith." Today, the gem we call jasper is an opaque, red quartz. But in John's day, jasper must have referred to a different stone, because he says it was "clear as crystal" (see Rev. 21:11). The believer's faith, like this gem, should be crystal clear.

2.) Sapphire is "the height of celestial hope." The brilliant blue of this gemstone represents heaven.

3.) Chalcedony is a translucent form of quartz, sometimes with a tint of yellow or red, resembling a flame. Maurus said this stone represents "the flame of inner charity."

4.) Emerald: "Strong faith in adversity." The beautiful green emerald reminds us of our vibrant, living faith.

5.) Sardonyx symbolizes "the humility of saints." This "humble" gem is a type of onyx layered with bands of red and white. Sardonyx is beautiful, but not "flashy" like the other jewels listed.

6.) Sardius, a red quartz stone, is an excellent symbol for "the blood of martyrs."

7.) Maurus said that chrysolite symbolizes "spiritual preaching accompanied by miracles." Chrysolite is the yellow form of the gem olivine. In John's time, and even today, the principle source of chrysolite is an island in the Red Sea, the site of one of the major miracles of the Bible. (See Exod. 14.)

8.) Beryl: "The perfect operation of prophecy." This dazzling jewel was featured prominently in Daniel's prophetic vision (Dan. 10:5–6) and Ezekiel's vision of the "four living creatures" (Ezek. 1:16, 10:9). (See Element 4, beryllium).

9.) Topaz. Maurus said that this yellow jewel represents the "ardent contemplation of prophecies."

10.) Chrysoprase. This stone is thought to be an apple-yellow form of chalcedony. Maurus said it symbolizes the "work and reward of the martyrs."

11.) Jacinth or zircon was the hardest and most brilliant stone known to John. (Only the diamond is harder, but Bible scholars say that true diamonds were unknown in those days.) Bishop Maurus believed that the diamond-like qualities of this gem represented "the celestial rapture of the learned in their high thoughts."

12.) Amethyst represents the "constant thought of the heavenly kingdom in humble souls," according to Maurus. How appropriate that this beautifully clear, purple stone, like the twilight sky on a clear night, should be associated with the contemplation of God's kingdom. Every evening when the busy day is done, our thoughts should turn to God and His kingdom and the blessings that await the believer.

REACTION: *THE TWELVE APOSTLES OF THE LAMB*

Now the wall of the city had twelve foundations, and on them were the names of the twelve apostles of the Lamb (Rev. 21:14).

The heavenly city of Jerusalem, as John described it, is a city of "twelves" (Rev. 21). The city had 12 gates, guarded by 12 angels. On the gates were written the names of the 12 tribes of Israel. There were also 12 foundation stones covered with the gems described above. On the foundations were written the names of the "twelve apostles of the Lamb."

JUST WHO WERE THESE 12 APOSTLES?

The Bible lists Jesus' inner core of 12 followers in three places: Matthew 10:3, Mark 3:18, and Luke 6:14. All of these lists include Judas Iscariot. The list of disciples in Acts 1:13 contains only 11, of course, because by this time, Judas had killed himself. Even though Judas was one of "the twelve" chosen by Jesus, surely as a traitor his name would not be on one of the heavenly foundations.

Peter thought it was extremely important to restore their number to 12 after Judas' betrayal. So they narrowed their choices down to two men who had followed Jesus with them from the beginning. They felt these two were equally qualified, so they asked God to help them choose and they "cast lots." (Casting lots was similar to rolling dice or drawing straws. The disciples trusted God to make the outcome right.) The one chosen was Matthias (Acts 1:15–26).

But some people say the disciples were too hasty. They say that Paul was really Judas' replacement. Jesus himself chose Paul on the road to Damascus (Acts 9:6), just as He had chosen the original 12. If only they had waited awhile, they would have known. Surely Paul, who started so many churches, wrote so much of the New Testament, and performed so many miracles — surely his name should be on one of the 12 foundation stones. After all, Matthias was only chosen by a "roll of the dice."

Paul even claimed the title of "Apostle" several times in his writings. Matthias, after his selection, is never heard from again in the Bible. (However, church tradition says that Matthias went on to preach in Judea and died there as a martyr.)

But Paul never claimed such an honor for himself, to be one of "the twelve." He thought of himself as "less than the least of all the saints" (Eph. 3:8). Although forgiven by God, he could never forget his terrible actions against the Church, including those he executed. ("For I am the least of the apostles, who am not worthy to be called an apostle, because I persecuted the church of God" [1 Cor. 15:9].) And in 1 Corinthians 15:5, Paul implicitly endorses Peter's choice of Matthias by referring to "the twelve" who saw the resurrected Christ.

Whether or not his name is written on the twelfth foundation stone, certainly Paul was content that his name is written in the "Book of Life" (Phil. 4:3).

QUICK QUIZ

1. Zirconium is a _____ metal.

   a. soft   b. tough   c. yellow   d. easily corroded

2. The gem called zircon most closely resembles what other precious stone due to its hardness?

   a. pearl   b. ruby   c. diamond   d. beryl

3. Zircon is also called jacinth or hyacinth, and it adorns one of the 12 foundation stones of the heavenly city of _____.

   a. Jerusalem   b. Jericho   c. Babylon   d. Damascus

4. In Acts chapter 1, the disciples chose _____ to replace Judas.

   a. Paul   b. Peter   c. Matthias   d. no one

5. Why did Paul call himself "the least of the apostles"?

   a. he was the last one   b. he persecuted Christians   c. he was short   d. he was young

RESPONSE

Who do you think belongs on the 12th foundation stone (the stone of amethyst): Matthias or Paul?

| 41 |
| **Nb** |
| 92.9064 |

NIOBIUM: "The Element with Two Names"

"To him who overcomes I will give ... a new name written, which no one knows except him who receives it" (Rev. 2:17).

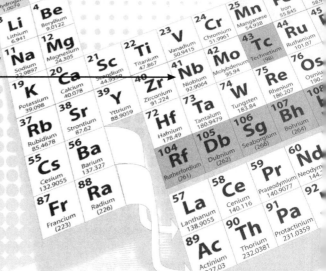

DATA

> Niobium is a shiny, white, soft, ductile metal.

> Niobium was once considered to be rare, but now significant quantities are generated as by-products of the production of other metals.

> Niobium's compounds have few commercial applications, but as a pure metal or in alloys, it is becoming increasingly useful: in forms of stainless steel, in eyeglasses, and in welding.

> Niobium is named after Niobe, the daughter of Tantalus in Greek mythology.

> It was discovered by Charles Hatchett of England in 1801, in an ore originally found in Connecticut.

ANALYSIS

Niobium or Columbium? That is the question!

COLUMBIUM. The English chemist Charles Hatchett (1765–1847) was a prolific scientist. He wrote some of the earliest studies on the chemical composition of teeth, seashells, and bones. He also did early studies of biological gels: mucus, egg whites, etc. In 1801, he began a study of some mineral samples that had been long-abandoned in the British Museum in London. These rocks had originally been sent to England by an American colonist, John Winthrop, who had died many years earlier. Winthrop (1681–1747) was the grandson of the first colonial governor of Massachusetts. He had studied many of the rocks of New England. He shipped samples of some of the most interesting ones to England for further study.

The sample that Hatchett found to be the most interesting was "a very heavy black stone, with golden streaks," which Winthrop had found in Connecticut. No similar mineral had yet been found and Winthrop named it "columbite" after Columbus, since as far as he knew it might only exist in the New World. When Charles Hatchett analyzed the mineral, he determined that it contained a new element, a metal, which he called columbium in honor of Winthrop's original discovery. He gave it the chemical symbol Cb.

NIOBIUM. Despite Charles Hatchett's reputation, people forgot about columbium over the years. In 1846 a German chemist, Heinrich Rose, was studying a substance that was chemically very similar to another element, tantalum (no. 73). Rose was convinced that he had discovered a new element himself, and he named it "niobium" after the Greek goddess Niobe, who was the daughter of Tantalus (after whom "tantalum" had been named).

Eventually, scientists proved that "columbium" and "niobium" were actually the same element, so credit for its discovery should rightly have gone to Charles Hatchett, who discovered it first. Unfortunately, by this time the name "niobium" had really caught on in Europe, while "columbium" was used uniformly in North America.

THE VERDICT. The controversy over the name of element no. 41 would continue for a century until the International Union of Pure and Applied Chemistry (IUPAC), the body that governs the naming of chemicals, met in 1950. IUPAC was dominated by Europeans at the time and they chose niobium as the official name. However, many leading metallurgists and most American commercial producers still refer to the metal by its original name "columbium," in honor of its discovery in America and the discoverer of the original mineral, John Winthrop of Massachusetts.

So element 41 continues to be the element with two names.

REACTION: *A NEW NAME*

Many of the most important figures in the Bible also had two names. Often God gave His chosen leaders a new name to correspond with a new mission or phase in their lives.

GENESIS 17:5: *"No longer shall your name be called Abram, but your name shall be Abraham."* Abram meant "exalted father" in Hebrew, but God changed his name to mean "the father of a multitude" in honor of His covenant with Abraham.

GENESIS 17:15–16: *"As for Sarai your wife, you shall not call her name Sarai, but Sarah shall be her name.... Then I will bless her, and she shall be a mother of nations."* Sarah's old name meant "The Lord is a prince," but her new name meant "princess."

GENESIS 32:28: *"Your name shall no longer be called Jacob, but Israel; for you have struggled with God and with men, and have prevailed."* Jacob, whose name meant "quarreler," was given a new name meaning "the prince of God." Israel would continue to be the name of the Jewish people and official name of the Jewish state.

JOHN 1:42: *"You are Simon the son of Jonah. You shall be called Cephas...."* Simon Peter was Jesus' most prominent disciple. Jesus gave him the Aramaic name Cephas, which means "rock." Cephas is translated into Greek as Petros, or as we now say, Peter.

ACTS 13:9: *"Then Saul, who also is called Paul, filled with the Holy Spirit, looked intently at him."* The apostle Paul seems to have changed his own Hebrew name to the Greek name "Paul" (meaning "little" or "short") in order to minister more effectively to the Gentiles.

---

1. Niobium was first found in rocks from _____.

    a. Connecticut   b. Ohio   c. England   d. Utah

2. Many scientists, especially in America, refer to niobium as _____.

    a. tantalum   b. columbium   c. magellum   d. aluminum

3. Which biblical character was not given a new name by God?

    a. Abraham   b. Sarah   c. Lot   d. Jacob

4. One of Jesus' disciples, Simon, was renamed Peter, which means _____.

    a. rock   b. trumpet   c. church   d. fisherman

5. Niobium is generally produced as a _____ of the production of other metals.

RESPONSE

To him who overcomes I will give some of the hidden manna to eat. And I will give him a white stone, and on the stone a new name written which no on knows except him who receives it (Revelation 2:17.)

The theme verse is from Christ's messages to the seven churches. Jesus promises that if we overcome the temptations and corruption of the world around us, we will someday receive a new name, like Abraham, Sarah, and other servants of God, befitting our own character and service.

"God, help me to overcome the world and in so doing honor You and receive the blessings that You promise to Your servants. Amen."

42
Mo
95.94

MOLYBDENUM and the Trace Minerals

"I will praise You, for I am fearfully and wonderfully made; marvelous are Your works, and that my soul knows very well" (Ps. 139:14).

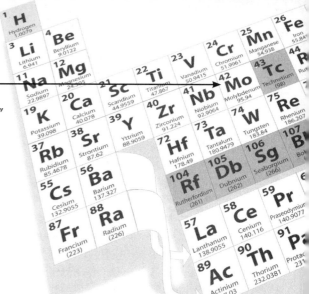

DATA

> Molybdenum is a silvery-white, hard metal, similar to tungsten but softer.

> The name comes from the Greek word *molybdos* meaning "lead."

> Working together the Swedish chemists Carl Scheele and Peter Hjelm isolated molybdenum around 1781.

> Before molybdenum's discovery, molybdenum compounds were often confused with compounds of lead.

> Molybdenum is used to make "moly steel," an important alloy used to make guns and cannons.

> Trace amounts of molybdenum are vital for life and health. However, it is toxic in high doses.

ANALYSIS

In Darwin's time, living things were thought to be made of fairly simple combinations of carbon, oxygen, hydrogen, and a few other elements. Cell theory (one of the first hints to the complexity of life) had not yet been developed. Most people, including evolutionary scientists, believed in the idea of the "spontaneous generation" of simple life forms (likes worms, flies, germs, etc.) from non-living things. So the Darwinian concept that early forms of life developed spontaneously was easy for many to accept.

However, as our understanding of the complexity of biology grew, it became necessary for evolutionary scientists to try to explain how life could have developed by strictly natural processes. In 1953 Stanley Miller and Harold Urey devised a process to manufacture simple amino acids from a mixture of methane, ammonia, hydrogen, and water. Their experiment was lauded as a breakthrough and the first step in creating life in the laboratory. In fact, all they succeeded in producing were tiny amounts of the two simplest amino acids: glycine and alanine. (Complex chains of all 22 amino acids are needed to make even rudimentary proteins.)

To date, this type of experiment has only proven that a high degree of intelligence and a sophisticated lab are needed to make simple organic molecules.

In fact, the situation is even more difficult for evolutionists. Every cell of every living thing is a tiny, incredibly complex manufacturing plant for producing thousands (perhaps millions) of organic molecules. And life depends not just on the so-called elements of life: carbon, hydrogen, oxygen, nitrogen, and sulfur.

At least 25 elements are known to be essential for humans. Most, if not all, of these are required for all life: bacteria, plants, and animals. Single-cell organisms, the supposed evolutionary ancestors of all living things, are not just simple sacs of organic molecules, but incredibly complex life forms.

ESSENTIAL TRACE MINERALS. In the Table of Essential Elements to the right, the elements from copper to cobalt are considered trace minerals. They exist in the body at levels of one part per million (ppm) or less. But if any one of them were to be removed from your body, you would die within minutes.

Molybdenum, 22nd on the list, makes up only 0.1 ppm of your body, but it performs dozens of vital functions. Around 20 known enzymes have molybdenum as their crucial ingredient. Molybdenum, based enzymes are found in all life forms and are indispensable to the nitrogen-fixing bacteria (see element 7, nitrogen). Molybdenum has functions in our bones, skin, liver, and kidneys. It is known to be required for the formation of urine, digestion of proteins and alcohol, strengthening of dental enamel, and the production of energy.

REACTION: *HOW THE BONES GROW*

As you do not know what is the way of the wind, or how the bones grow in the womb of her who is with child, so you do not know the works of God who makes everything (Eccles. 11:5).

The role of trace elements, like molybdenum, in the human body was largely unknown before the late 20th century. But with the advance of technology, we continue to discover more and more of the incredible complexity of God's design for life.

As just one example, we can now begin to appreciate the role of trace elements with regard to fetal development, or as Solomon said in the verse above, "How the bones grow in the womb." Tin, copper, and even vanadium are all known to be vital for proper growth of the unborn child. Iodine is especially needed during the first three months of pregnancy for the development of the nervous system and brain. (This is one reason that table salt is "iodized" or fortified with iodine.) And scientists do not yet know why, but the organ of the human body with the highest levels of chromium is the placenta.

The following is a list of just a few of the known roles for trace elements in the human body:

> Copper: in at least 10 enzymes, to produce energy, repair connective tissue, and make melanin

> Selenium: hormone production in the thyroid gland, key enzymes, etc

> Vanadium: regulation of sodium levels in the body

> Chromium: control of blood sugar and cholesterol levels

Since most or all of these trace elements are required for even the simplest forms of life, we also see plainly the bankruptcy of the theory of evolution to explain the origins of life.

ELEMENTS KNOWN TO BE ESSENTIAL FOR HUMAN LIFE:*

1. Oxygen	14. Fluorine
2. Carbon	15. Zinc
3. Hydrogen	16. Copper
4. Nitrogen	17. Manganese
5. Calcium	18. Tin
6. Phosphorus	19. Iodine
7. Sulfur	20. Selenium
8. Potassium	21. Nickel
9. Sodium	22. Molybdenum
10. Chlorine	23. Vanadium
11. Magnesium	24. Chromium
12. Silicon	25. Cobalt
13. Iron	

• In order by percent of body weight.

Other possible essential elements: arsenic, barium, boron, bromine, cadmium, and lithium.

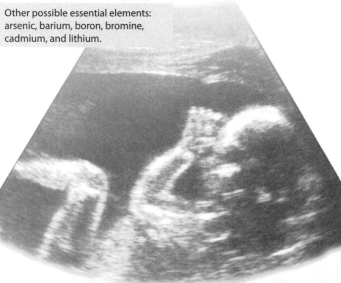

QUICK QUIZ

1. Molybdenum was originally confused with what similar metal?

2. Moly steel is used to produce what products?

    a. guns   b. spacecraft   c. spark plugs   d. computers

3. Molybdenum is vital for _____.

    a. good health   b. televisions   c. rubber tires   d. fiberglass

4. At least _____ elements are needed for human life.

    a. 5   b. 10   c. 25   d. 50

5. Elements that are needed for human life, but only in very small amounts, are called _____ elements. (Fill in the blank.)

RESPONSE

Of course, known roles for these minerals probably only scratch the surface. And we are likely to find that several other elements are essential for life. For in biology, as in most areas of science, the more we learn about the chemistry of the human body, the more questions we have. And the more there is to learn.

Science may never learn all the secrets of "how fearfully and wonderfully" we are made.

"Heavenly Father, thank You for our daily bread and the nutrition that provides our energy and health and physical growth. Let me use that strength and health to honor You in every moment of my life. As I learn more of the wonders of our created world, Lord, help me never to take Your gifts for granted. In Jesus name, Amen."

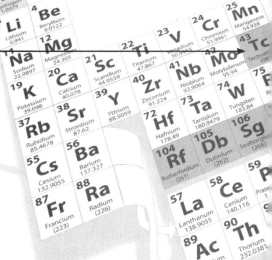

43
Tc
(98)*

TECHNETIUM: "Something New under the Sun?"

"That which has been is what will be, that which is done is what will be done, and there is nothing new under the sun" (Eccles. 1:9).

DATA

> Technetium was the first man-made element. (*The atomic weight listed is that of technetium's most stable isotope.)

> It is a corrosion-resistant, silvery metal (but it is most commonly produced as a gray powder).

> Technetium's name comes from the Greek word *technetos*, meaning "artificial."

> In 1937 Italian chemists Emilio Gino Segre and Carlos Perrier isolated element 43, which had been predicted by Mendeleev but was missing from the periodic table at that time.

> Originally produced only in microscopic amounts, today technetium is created by the tons every year in spent nuclear fuel rods.

ANALYSIS

In the Book of Ecclesiastes, Solomon wrote, "There is nothing new under the sun." The writer's statement refers to the futility of life when lived on a secular, earthly level, a life lived without God as one's first priority. (The phase "under the sun" appears 29 times in Ecclesiastes.) Solomon seems to view secular life as a big soap opera, which he calls "vanity of vanities" (Eccles. 1:2). Nothing ever really changes. History just repeats itself. There is nothing new under the sun. One might wonder: Does Solomon's statement also apply to the chemical elements? Can man create a totally new element?

Ever since Mendeleev predicted the structure of the periodic table (see element 31, gallium), scientists had been trying to fill in the blank squares. By the 1930s, it was clear there was a major hole at element 43. Some believed that it would never be found because it did not exist. After all, no rule said that every box had to be filled. Others thought the element might be so rare that it could not be found. Soon these questions would be answered.

In 1936 American physicist Ernest Lawrence of the University of California-Berkeley fired a beam of radiation (actually deuterons or "heavy hydrogen" nuclei) at a piece of molybdenum foil for several months. The foil became radioactive. Lawrence sent the foil to Emilio Segre at the University of Palermo, Italy. (Lawrence may have been trying to recruit Segre. In fact, Segre came to UC Berkeley in 1938 to escape Mussolini's fascist regime.) Segre estimated that about one ten-billionth of a gram of a new element had been created. Segre was soon able to prove that it was element 43, which he named "technetium." The new element had been created according to the following nuclear reaction:

Molybdenum-96 + Hydrogen-2 → Technetium-97 + Neutron
(42 protons/54 neutrons) (1proton/1 neutron) (43 protons/54 neutrons) (1 neutron)

So it appeared that, yes, at least as far as the elements were concerned, there was something "new under the sun." Technetium! However, in 1940 Segre himself found that small amounts of technetium existed naturally in uranium deposits. This is due to a totally natural nuclear process that has been going on ever since creation. In a sense, man had just copied the natural process in a physics laboratory.

Likewise, other "man-made" elements, like promethium (61), astatine (85), and francium (87), were eventually found in exceedingly small quantities in nature, after they were created in labs. Even the super-heavy man-made elements (elements 93 and above) have either been found in nature or they are believed to exist in nature, at least in very minute amounts, due to natural radioactivity. Perhaps, even in the periodic table, there truly is "nothing new under the sun."

REACTION: *A NEW CREATION*

Therefore, if anyone is in Christ, he is a new creation; old things have passed away; behold, all things have become new (2 Cor. 5:17).

In Solomon's eyes there was "no new thing under the sun." He lamented man's tendency to repeat the sins of the past. Solomon had repeated some of his father's bad choices, and his own son was making worse ones. Solomon tried to convince his readers of the futility of worldly pleasures, power, and riches, as ends in themselves. Finally, he exhorted his readers to "Remember now your Creator in the days of your youth, before difficult days come" (Eccles. 12:1).

But in 2 Corinthians 5:17, Paul says we all have a choice about how to live our lives. We don't have to live "under the sun." Instead we can live "in Christ."

IN CHRIST

In the Book of John, Jesus tells His disciples to "abide in Me." He says that those who abide in Him will "have peace" (John 16:33), will be productive (15:5), and will have their prayers answered (15:7).

Paul's writings frequently use the phrase "in Christ" to describe the close "positional" relationship that believers have with Jesus. When we are "in Christ," we are surrounded by His love and covered by His forgiveness. Here are some blessings that Paul said come from being in Christ:

> In Christ, there is no condemnation (Romans 8:1) or division (Galatians 3:28). In Christ, we have sanctification (1 Corinthians 1:2); wisdom (1 Corinthians 4:10); and salvation (2 Timothy 2:10).

NEW CREATION

If you are in Christ, you are a "new creation." You are "born again," as Jesus puts it in John chapter 3. Through this new birth and remaining in Christ, you can break out of the futility of life "under the sun." God is the loving Father and He knows our hearts and our needs even better than we do. As a Christian you can rely on the Spirit of God for guidance and comfort. And best of all, as new creatures in Christ, we have eternal life.

> *For as in Adam all die, even so in Christ shall all be made alive* (I Corinthians 15:22).

QUICK QUIZ

1. Technetium was the first _____ element. (Fill in the blank.)

2. The existence of technetium was predicted by _____.

    a. Sir Humphry Davy   b. Aristotle   c. the Bible   d. Dmitri Mendeleev

3. Solomon wrote that "there is nothing _____ under the sun."

    a. safe   b. pale   c. dark   d. new

4. Originally, microscopic quantities of technetium were made by bombarding a piece of what metal with radiation?

    a. molybdenum   b. lead   c. gold   d. magnesium

5. Today tons of technetium are generated every year from the processing of nuclear _____ _____. (Fill in the blanks.)

RESPONSE

"Lord, it is so easy for me to get bogged down by the world and the pressures of living. In Christ, my Savior, I know that I can have an abundant life, since You have made me a new creature through Him. Help me to share this new life with others so that they might be brought into Your Kingdom as well. Amen."

44
Ru
101.07

RUTHENIUM and the Platinum Group

"The law of Your mouth is better to me than thousands of coins of gold and silver" (Ps. 119:72).

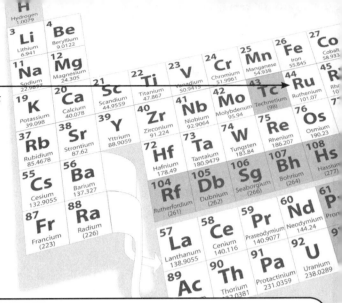

DATA

> Ruthenium is a rare, brittle, silvery metal, with many similarities to platinum.

> It was isolated by the chemist Karl Karlovich Klaus in 1844. He named it in honor of his home country, Russia. (Ruthenia was the Latin name for Russia.)

> Most platinum jewelry contains about 2 percent ruthenium.

> By their order in the periodic table, ruthenium is the first element of the group of six metals known as the "platinum group," but it was the last of the group to be discovered.

PLATINUM GROUP

Ru	Rh	Pd
Os	Ir	Pt

ANALYSIS

Beginning as early as 1557, European explorers described a shiny new silver—like metal found in the New World. The native Central Americans used it for jewelry and decorations. The Spaniards who had conquered the area knew that it was different from silver, because they could not melt it, even at temperatures much higher than silver's melting point. They called this new metal *platina,* meaning "little silver" or "silvery" (which, of course, is where the name "platinum" comes from).

1750   PLATINUM IDENTIFIED

As samples of this New World metal began to make their way to Europe, interest in it among chemists became intense. William Watson of England identified platinum as a new metal in 1750. Many scientific greats, such as Lavoisier of France (the Father of Modern Chemistry), Berzelius of Sweden (the discoverer of cesium, selenium, silicon, and thorium), and Marggraf of Germany (who had isolated zinc) studied it. But even these brilliant men did not discover that "platinum" was really a mix of six elements. That would not occur until the 19th century.

1803   PALLADIUM AND RHODIUM

The Englishman William Hyde Wollaston retired as a medical doctor in 1800, due to failing eyesight. He moved to London to devote his time to the study of chemistry. Fifty years after being identified as an element, platinum still had few uses. Its high melting point and resistance to chemical reactions made it difficult to work with. However, Wollaston found a way to make it malleable and developed strong acids to dissolve it. Using these acids, in 1803 he discovered that natural platinum contained small amounts of two similar metals, which he named palladium and rhodium. Wollaston's work with platinum made him wealthy and famous. He went on to research other areas of chemistry, as well as diabetes and gout.

1804   IRIDIUM AND OSMIUM

Wollaston's close friend, fellow physician, and former classmate, Smithson Tennant, was also working on platinum in London. Within a year after Wollaston's discoveries, Tennant discovered the next two platinum group members, which he called iridium and osmium. Tennant likewise became a respected chemist and researcher.

1844   RUTHENIUM

Mendeleev's periodic table was still a few decades in the future, so no one suspected that there was still a missing platinum-like element. But with the discovery of platinum ore in Russia's Ural Mountains in 1822, a new elemental discoverer came on the scene. The Russian chemist Karl Karlovich Klaus had become an expert on platinum. Chemists from all over Europe sought him out for his knowledge. In 1844, Klaus discovered the Russian member of the Platinum family, and he proudly named it ruthenium in honor of his home country.

REACTION: *MORE PRECIOUS THAN GOLD*

In modern society, if something is said to be more valuable than gold or silver, it's probably platinum. Platinum and other platinum group metals are all rarer than gold and more valuable. Platinum is increasingly popular as jewelry, often alloyed with iridium or other platinum group metals to increase hardness. Items referred to as "white gold" are actually a mixture of gold and palladium. Popular record albums were once referred to as "silver" or "gold records," depending on the number sold, but as the record industry grew a new term was needed: "platinum records."

But when the Bible speaks of things "more precious than silver and gold," it is referring to spiritual things:

THE COMMANDMENTS OF THE LORD

David tells us that keeping God's commands is "more to be desired . . . than gold, yea, than much fine gold" (Ps. 19:10. See also Ps. 119:72 and 119:127).

GODLY WISDOM

The wisdom of God is better than "silver . . . choice gold . . . [or] rubies." In fact, "All the things one may desire cannot be compared with [wisdom]" (Prov. 8:10–11. See also Prov. 3:13–14, 8:19, and 16:16).

EVEN THE RICHEST MAN CANNOT BUY WISDOM

The Book of Job even contains a list of the precious metals and gems that do not compare with the value of wisdom: gold, silver, onyx, sapphire, crystal, coral, rubies, and topaz (Job 28:12–19).

FAITH, NOT RICHES, LEADS TO SALVATION

Finally, Peter tells us that genuine faith is "much more precious than gold that perishes" because only faith will result in our soul's salvation and eternal life (1 Pet. 1:6–9)!

QUICK QUIZ

1. Ruthenium is the first member of the _____ _____ of metals. (Fill in the blanks.)

2. Platinum was discovered in _____.

   a. Central America   b. Russia   c. China   d. Canada

3. Ruthenium was first found in _____.

   a. Central America   b. Russia   c. China   d. Canada

4. The Bible says that faith, wisdom, and God's commandments are all more precious than _____. (Just like platinum.)

   a. food   b. love   c. gold   d. happiness

5. Platinum is similar to silver but it has a much higher _____.

   a. pH   b. conductivity   c. melting point   d. atomic weight

RESPONSE

"Lord, help me to set the right priorities is my life. Riches cannot save my soul. Money cannot buy me happiness. Gold, silver, and platinum mean nothing to me if I am not following You and being faithful to Your Word. I ask for Your wisdom that is more valuable than anything I can imagine. Thank You for Your patience as I try to walk the path You have set before me. I know that everything I entrust to You will be kept safe and that one day I will see You face to face in a land where gold is as common as the dust in the street, and Your blessing is the only thing of value. In Christ's name, Amen."

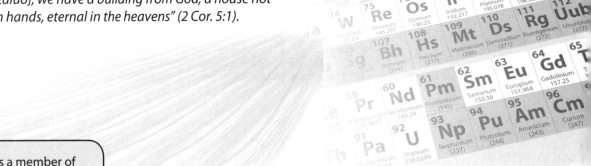

45
Rh
102.9055

RHODIUM: "The Catalytic Converter"

"For we know that if our earthly house, this tent, is destroyed [Greek cataluo], we have a building from God, a house not made with hands, eternal in the heavens" (2 Cor. 5:1).

DATA

> Rhodium is a member of the platinum group of metals. It is usually found in platinum ore, and it is chemically similar to platinum.

> Rhodium is hard, silvery, and lustrous.

> Rhodium was discovered in 1803 by the English chemist William Hyde Wollaston as a minor component of a platinum specimen he was testing.

> He named the new metal "rhodium" (from the Greek *rhodon*, meaning "rose-colored") due to the rose-red crystals of rhodium chloride ($RhCl_3$) he created.

> Some high-quality silverware is electroplated with rhodium to prevent tarnishing.

> Like the other platinum group metals, rhodium is useful as an industrial catalyst.

William Hyde Wollaston

ANALYSIS

Like many of the terms used by scientists, the word "catalyst" is from the Greek language. Catalyst comes from the word *cataluo* (pronounced CAT-a-LOO-oh), which has various meanings in Greek. In the verse quoted above, 2 Corinthians 5:1, it means to "destroy" or "break down." It can also mean to "bring about a change," and that is the meaning of the word as used in the science.

A catalyst is a substance that, just by being present, changes how fast a chemical reaction occurs, while the catalyst itself is unchanged. Since catalysts are unaffected by the reaction, they can be re-used almost indefinitely. Catalysts are very important in industry and are used to make many of the things we use in everyday life. Here are a few examples:

> Iron is used as a catalyst in the "Haber process" to combine nitrogen and hydrogen gas to make ammonia for fertilizer.

> A copper-based catalyst is used to convert hydrogen and carbon monoxide to make methanol, an important industrial chemical.

> Other metallic catalysts are used to convert vegetable oils into vegetable shortening.

PLATINUM GROUP METALS AS CATALYSTS

Some of the most promising new catalysts are now being found among the platinum group metals. They are increasingly used in refining of crude oil, improving gasoline, and synthesizing organic chemicals. Despite their high cost, since only small quantities of catalyst are needed and they are not used up in the reaction, the use of platinum metal catalysts is very cost effective. However, it is in the area of pollution control that the platinum metals, especially rhodium, really shine!

PLATINUM GROUP		
Ru	Rh	Pd
Os	Ir	Pt

As pollution and energy conservation have become more important in modern life, the role of rhodium has really come to the forefront. About 16 tons of rhodium are produced per year. About 85 percent of the annual production of rhodium is used to make catalytic converters for cars and trucks.

Catalytic converters are devices that change pollutant gasses in car exhausts, like excess gasoline and carbon monoxide, into harmless water vapor and carbon dioxide. A porous block of rhodium in the converter acts as the catalyst. This tough, temperature-resistant, but expensive platinum group metal plays an important role in protecting the environment.

REACTION: *CATALYTIC CONVERSION*

So, being sent on their way by the church, [Paul and Barnabas] passed through Phoenicia and Samaria, describing the conversion of the Gentiles; and they caused great joy to all the brethren (Acts 15:3).

A catalyst causes things to happen just by its presence. A catalyst does not change from the reaction, but it causes change in others.

In the Sermon on the Mount, Jesus called for His followers to be "the salt of the earth" and "the light of the world" (Matthew 5:13-16). Salt preserves and improves. Light clears away darkness and lights a path. Yet neither salt nor light change their nature as they do their work.

Conversion is a process of changing one thing into something totally different.

In the Great Commission (Matthew 28:19), Jesus said, "Go therefore and make disciples of all the nations, baptizing them in the name of the Father and of the Son and of the Holy Spirit."

Christians are called to be "catalytic converters," making disciples wherever we go.

QUICK QUIZ

1. Rhodium and the platinum group metals are known for their properties as catalysts. Define catalyst.

2. About 85 percent of all rhodium produced is used to make catalytic converters for_____.

   a. cars and trucks   b. food production   c. making gasoline   d. air conditioning

3. TRUE or FALSE: Catalysts can be re-used almost indefinitely.

4. The rhodium in catalytic converters removes excess gasoline and _____ _____ from vehicle exhaust. (Fill in the blanks.)

   a. carbon dioxide   b. carbon monoxide   c. battery acid   d. lead oxide

5. In Acts 15:3 Paul and Barnabas reported on what event that caused "great joy among the brethren"?

RESPONSE

"Lord, help me to represent You well in the world so that I might lead others into the knowledge of salvation. Help me to keep myself, pure and unchanged by the sinful influences of society. In Jesus name. Amen."

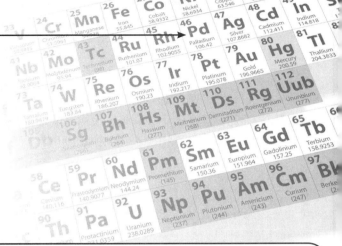

46
Pd
106.42

PALLADIUM: "The Hydrogen Sponge"

"Those who were foolish took their lamps and took no oil with them, but the wise took oil in their vessels with their lamps" (Matt. 25:3–4).

DATA

> Palladium is a lustrous, silvery white, malleable, and ductile metal.

> Palladium is a member of the platinum group of metals. It is chemically similar to platinum.

> Palladium was discovered in 1803 by the English chemist William Hyde Wollaston as a minor component of a platinum specimen he was testing.

> He named the new metal after Pallas, an asteroid discovered in 1802. The asteroid was named for the Greek goddess of wisdom, Pallas Athena.

> Like the other platinum group metals, palladium is useful as an industrial catalyst.

> Palladium is especially good at absorbing hydrogen.

PLATINUM GROUP

Ru	Rh	Pd
Os	Ir	Pt

ANALYSIS

Modern society relies on gasoline and other hydrocarbons for fuel. Coal, oil, and natural gas fuel our power plants. Gasoline stations are ubiquitous in our cities and towns. Even with increasing oil prices, petroleum-based fuels are still the most energy-efficient, practical, and inexpensive forms of energy available.

However, some scientists and political leaders predict that within decades we will transition into a "hydrogen economy." They say that hydrogen will be the fuel of the future. It certainly has some advantages.

1. NO POLLUTION. Hydrogen combines with oxygen to produce energy, via the equation $2H_2 + O_2 \rightarrow 2H_2O$. The only waste product is water vapor.

2. ENERGY OUTPUT. On a weight-for-weight basis, hydrogen generates about twice as much energy as hydrocarbons.

3. TRANSPORTATION AND BULK STORAGE. Hydrogen can easily be transferred in interstate pipelines. Vast amounts can be stored in underground caverns.

Someday, "hydrogen stations" may replace gas stations for fueling cars. However, before that happens, some major drawbacks must be addressed. First, inexpensive means of generating sufficient quantities of hydrogen must be found. (Today, hydrogen is much more expensive than gasoline.)

Next, a practical hydrogen storage tank for cars must be designed. Gasoline is a liquid that can safely be contained and refueled. But hydrogen is an explosive gas. Currently, in order to store sufficient quantities to fuel an automobile, hydrogen would have to be stored under very high pressure or even liquefied. To see the danger of such a means of storage, one must only look to the 1986 *Challenger* Space Shuttle disaster caused by a hydrogen fuel tank explosion.

But a solution to this quandary may come in the form of palladium. Palladium is unique among the elements in its ability to soak up hydrogen like a sponge! Imagine a single kitchen sponge that can soak up 100 gallons of water. That's similar to what palladium does when exposed to hydrogen. A 10-gallon "gas tank" filled with palladium (probably in the form of a mesh screen) could easily absorb more than 1,000 cubic feet of hydrogen. (That's the size of a room 10 feet long, 10 feet wide, and 10 feet high.) The individual hydrogen atoms (very tiny compared to the palladium atoms) appear to be drawn deep into the core of the metal, and the hydrogen is stored safely at low pressure.

If efficient ways can be developed to transfer the stored hydrogen to the car's engine for combustion, palladium could well be the key to the so-called Hydrogen Highway of the future.

REACTION: *THE WISE AND FOOLISH BRIDESMAIDS*

Now five of them were wise, and five were foolish (Matt. 25:2.)

When Jesus described the Kingdom of Heaven in Matthew 25:1-13, he referred to a marriage custom of the day. He told of a story of ten virgins (or, as we might call them, bridesmaids) who were given an important job at a wedding. They were to stand outside the gate and await the arrival of the bridegroom. In doing so, they lighted the way for late-arriving guests. Their oil-burning lamps in the dark street would show the location of the wedding celebration. But Jesus said that five of the young women were foolish. They did not bring enough olive-oil fuel for their lamps. As it turned out, the groom was delayed and by about midnight the foolish girls had no oil. They had to leave their assigned duties to re-fill their lamps, and while they were away the groom arrived. The five wise maidens had prepared themselves with plenty of fuel and remained at their posts, and they entered with the groom to join the feast. The foolish bridesmaids had a different fate. When they returned the door was locked and they were left in the darkness.

This is a timeless lesson about responsibility and preparation. Many things change with history and progress, but the need for energy and reliable fuel supplies is something every society must plan for. In the time of Christ, oil from olives was a major energy source. Industrious merchants brought it into the cities and wise people made sure they had plenty of it for their lighting needs. There was no other source of light in homes or the dark streets. Now our oil comes from oil wells instead of olive presses, and we buy it from gas stations, not oil merchants. As individuals and as a society, we still cannot afford to take our energy needs for granted.

Today, there is an unwise pressure to prematurely turn away from reliable energy resources in favor of new unproven technologies, the development of which may be many years away. Summer blackouts and steep increases in energy and fuel costs are early warnings that we must prepare properly. Wise energy planning will determine whether we will be ready for the unexpected like the faithful bridesmaids or be left in the dark like the others.

QUICK QUIZ

1. Palladium is useful for the storage of what gas?

   a. chlorine b. oxygen c. ammonia d. hydrogen

2. Unlike burning fossil fuels, the combustion of hydrogen in an engine produces only _____ in the exhaust.

   a. air b. carbon c. helium d. water

3. Palladium was discovered by what English chemist?

4. The Bible says that faith, wisdom, and God's commandments are all more precious than _____. (Just like palladium and platinum.)

   a. power b. love c. gold d. happiness

5. Palladium and platinum are similar to silver but they have much higher _____.

   a. pH b. conductivities c. melting points d. atomic weights

RESPONSE

What spiritual lesson does the Parable of the Wise and Foolish Virgins teach?

The wedding celebration represents heaven, and the Bridegroom is Christ himself, "The Son of Man." (verse 13). The wise virgins represent believers who have prepared themselves to enter the "gates" of heaven with Jesus. The oil in their lamps? In scripture, oil is symbolic of God's Spirit—the holy oil that keeps the flame of our faith burning, and the fuel we need shine in a dark world. We can lead others to the "Wedding Supper of the Lamb" only if our lamps are full and lighted. The Bible says when Christ returns it will be at a time when we least expect Him—in the dark of night (See I Thess. 5:2). Will you be ready?

"Watch therefore, for you know neither the day nor the hour in which the Son of Man is coming," (Matthew 25:13.)

47
Ag
107.868

SILVER: "The Element of Redemption"

"The words of the LORD are pure words, like silver tried in a furnace of earth, purified seven times" (Ps. 12:6).

DATA

> Silver is one of the seven metals known since antiquity (along with iron, copper, gold, lead, tin, and mercury).

> Silver is the 66th most abundant element on earth, but it is ten times more common than gold.

> Silver is a malleable and ductile metal with a beautiful sheen when polished.

> Silver is resistant to most chemicals other than sulfur compounds. Over time, exposure to small amounts of sulfur dioxide in the air causes silver to tarnish.

> Its name comes from the Anglo-Saxon word *siolfur*. The symbol Ag is for the Latin word for silver, *argentum*. (This is similar to its Greek equivalent, *arguros*.)

ANALYSIS

Silver is mentioned over 300 times in the Bible. (In addition, in over 200 references to "money" in the Bible, the actual Greek or Hebrew word is "silver.") The first mention of this element is in Genesis 13:2. "Abram was very rich in livestock, in silver, and in gold." Six more verses describe Abraham's wealth in terms of silver. The next mention of silver appears in the story of Joseph.

THE PRICE OF A SLAVE

When Joseph's brothers, in their jealousy, decided to kill him, they threw him in a pit. But through God's providence, some merchants came by and purchased Joseph from them for 20 pieces of silver — the price of a slave. Joseph was then resold in Egypt, where he eventually rose from slavery to a position of great power. Years later, when Joseph's family was facing a famine, his brothers came to Egypt to buy grain. Joseph met with his brothers and they did not recognize him. He tested them by placing a cup made of silver among their belongings. (Perhaps he used silver as a reminder of their betrayal.) Later when they were found with the silver chalice, Joseph could have made slaves of them all. Instead, he used the situation to save his family and to reunite with them. Joseph forgave his brothers for their treachery and gave his innocent youngest brother 300 pieces of silver. (For Joseph's story, see Gen. 37–50.)

When he learned of his brothers' regret for what they did to him, Joseph said, "Do not therefore be grieved or angry with yourselves because you sold me here; for God sent me before you to preserve life" (Gen. 45:5).

THE PRICE OF BETRAYAL

Judas Iscariot, one of the 12 disciples, served as the treasurer of Jesus' ministry (John 13:29). He may have initially joined Jesus out of pure motives, for Peter referred to him as a "fallen apostle" in Acts 1:25. But Judas disagreed with Jesus about the handling of money, and even took money from the ministry for himself (John 12:4–7, and perhaps Matt. 26:7–10). Through his love of money, Satan caused Judas to betray Jesus to the Jewish priests and elders (Luke 22:3–6). The price of his betrayal was 30 pieces of silver (a price prophesied in Zech. 11:12–13). In the end, Judas could not live with his choice and he did not profit from it. He threw the silver at the priests' feet and hanged himself. The priests, not wanting to take back the blood money, used it to purchase a graveyard for the poor (Matt. 27:3–10).

As Paul wrote to Timothy, perhaps even recalling Judas' greed, treachery, and ultimate fate: "For the love of money [literally, 'love of silver' in the Greek] is a root of all kinds of evil, for which some have strayed from the faith in their greediness, and pierced themselves through with many sorrows" (1 Tim. 6:10).

REACTION: *THE SILVERSMITH*

[The Lord] will sit as a refiner and a purifier of silver; He will purify the sons of Levi, and purge them as gold and silver, that they may offer to the LORD an offering in righteousness (Mal. 3:3).

This remarkable verse gives us some insights into the purpose of suffering in the life of a believer in Christ.

It paints a picture of God as a craftsman: a silversmith sitting before a very hot fire. In His hands, He holds an iron cup containing crude silver ore. He holds the ore over the hottest part of the fire until the silver begins to liquefy. As He heats it, the impurities, known as "dross," separate and start to float to the surface. With tender care not to spill the silver or overheat it, the silversmith takes a small brush to sweep away the dross. After a while the silver becomes shiny and smooth.

God wants to purify us of the sin and evil in our lives — the dross that makes us dull and dingy, spiritually. God demands purity because He is pure: He is "like a refiner's fire." When life is easy and there are no pressures to deal with, we are mostly happy to live without making the hard choices necessary to grow. But God allows difficulties to come into our lives, like the heat of the fire, so that we will become pure.

How does a silversmith know when the silver is pure? When he looks on the shiny, liquid surface and sees a face: his own reflection shimmering in the molten metal. When all the dross is gone, he can see his own reflection.

God is looking for a reflection in our lives, too. When we turn to God in times of trial and allow Him to brush away the dross, we will begin to show an image: the likeness of Jesus Christ.

QUICK QUIZ

1. Silver is about _____ times more common than gold in the earth's surface.

   a. three   b. 10   c. 20   d. 100

2. Sulfur dioxide in the air causes silver to _____.

   a. glow   b. tarnish   c. melt   d. smell funny

3. In Genesis, Joseph was sold as a slave for _____ pieces of silver.

   a. three   b. 10   c. 20   d. 100

4. Sometimes in the Bible, the Greek or Hebrew word for silver is translated as _____.

   a. money   b. love   c. gold   d. happiness

5. A silversmith can tell when his molten silver is pure when he sees his own _____.

   a. breath   b. future   c. reflection   d. happiness

RESPONSE

"Thank You, Father, for I know that when difficulties come, You will use them for my good. You will cleanse me and take away the impurities in my life so that I may draw closer to You. I pray that my family and friends and all the people I deal with will be able to see the reflection of Your precious Son in me. Amen."

CADMIUM and the Heavy Metals

"Have mercy on me, O LORD, for I am weak;
O LORD heal me, for my bones are troubled" (Ps. 6:2).

DATA

> Cadmium is a silvery metal with a bluish tinge. It is soft enough to be cut with a knife.

> Cadmium is from the Greek name *kadmeia*, for the mineral calamine or zinc oxide. Cadmium is produced as a by-product of zinc manufacture.

> Cadmium was discovered by three different German chemists at about the same time in 1817, but credit is generally given to Friedrich Strohmeyer, the German inspector of pharmacies.

> Cadmium has several modern uses: rechargeable Ni-Cad (nickel-cadmium) batteries, cadmium plating of steel to resist saltwater corrosion, and cadmium-based pigments for artists, in colors with names like cadmium yellow, cadmium orange, cadmium red, etc.

> Cadmium is considered a poisonous, heavy metal.

ANALYSIS

If you asked chemists what the term "heavy metal" means, you are likely to get multiple answers. (Hopefully, none of them would be "a type of loud rock music"!) Heavy metal is a generic term used to refer to a variety of elements found in the environment that are bad for your health. Usually included in the heavy metals are lead, mercury, arsenic, and cadmium. Some add beryllium, chromium, antimony, copper, nickel, and selenium as well.

LEAD. Lead in the environment comes from both human-caused and natural sources, but most lead exposure comes from the foods we eat. Minute amounts of lead are taken up by many plants depending on the lead content of the soil. Man-caused sources of lead have been greatly reduced by the phase-out of leaded gasoline, lead paint, and lead plumbing. Some urban areas still have elevated lead levels in soil due to past lead use in gasoline. Lead exposure causes reduced intelligence and slowed mental development in children. It is considered a cumulative poison that collects in the bones.

MERCURY. We are constantly exposed to trace amounts of mercury, mostly through drinking water and breathing air. Environmental mercury occurs naturally from soil erosion and volcanic emissions. Man-made sources of mercury in the air include the burning of coal and oil, incineration of garbage (containing fluorescent lighting, batteries, etc.), and cremation of human remains (from dental fillings.) We can also be exposed to mercury in food, especially in ocean fish like tuna and swordfish. Mercury exposure can cause nervous system damage, especially in fetuses and young children.

ARSENIC. Arsenic is a metalloid, but it is usually listed with the heavy metals when discussing the environment. Arsenic is mostly released to the environment from the burning of coal and oil, which normally contain small amounts of arsenic. In some areas, naturally occurring arsenic in groundwater is a major threat. Forest fires are another source of arsenic in the atmosphere.

CADMIUM. You can see why the human body has a problem with cadmium by looking at the periodic table. Cadmium appears just below zinc, and their chemical reactions are very similar. Zinc is an essential element in the human body. It is needed for more than 200 enzymes, for everything from digestion to reproduction. When cadmium is taken into the body, it is treated like zinc, but where zinc is beneficial, cadmium is harmful. Cadmium accumulates in the body and can take decades to be excreted. Chronic exposure damages kidneys and testicles, and it can cause a painful bone disease, first diagnosed in Japan, called "itai-itai." (In Japanese, this is the equivalent to "ouch-ouch" in English.) Ninety percent of cadmium in the environment is human-caused, mostly as a by-product of lead and zinc processing.

REACTION: *THE TEMPLE OF THE HOLY SPIRIT*

Or do you not know that your body is the temple of the Holy Spirit who is in you, whom you have from God, and you are not your own? (1 Cor. 6:19).

Cadmium is present in so many foods that it is impossible to totally exclude it from our diets. The average person takes in from 0.1 to 1 micrograms of cadmium each day.

However, smokers can easily increase that exposure by 800 percent or more. Like many plants, tobacco is known to take up large amounts of cadmium from the soil into its leaves. Smoking two packs of cigarettes daily can lead to the inhalation of eight micrograms or more of cadmium each day. The body has ways of removing some of the cadmium taken into the digestive system, but inhaled cadmium enters directly into the bloodstream via the lungs and then to every organ of the body.

Traditionally, Christians have regarded cigarette smoking as sinful. A Christian who smokes exhibits a poor testimony that may keep others from turning to Christ. Smoking is poor stewardship, because of the money required to support the habit. Finally, the health effects of smoking are damaging to the body.

Cadmium is just another reminder that we should faithfully take care of our bodies: "the temple of the Holy Spirit."

1. Cadmium and nickel are used to make _____ batteries.

   a. car   b. AAA   c. Ni-Cad   d. dead

2. Cadmium is used to make several colors of _____.

   a. paints for artists   b. food coloring   c. fabric dyes   d. soft drinks

3. Ninety percent of the cadmium found in the environment is caused by _____.

   a. volcanoes   b. human activity   c. sea life   d. forest fires

4. Lead, mercury, arsenic, cadmium, and some other elements are often classified as _____ metals. (Fill in the blank.)

5. A healthy way that you can prevent high levels of cadmium from entering your body is to avoid _____.

   a. breathing   b. drinking   c. eating   d. smoking

RESPONSE

"Father, You have blessed me with life and breath; I will not waste it with unhealthy things, like tobacco. You have given me a way to earn a living; I will not squander my wages on sinful habits. You have called me to represent the True Light of salvation, to a lost and dying world; I won't deny my testimony with shameful self-indulgences. Help me to take Your Word seriously. My body is the temple of Your Spirit; let me treat it as such. Amen."

49
In
114.818

INDIUM: "The Purple Thread"

"Now a certain woman named Lydia heard us. She was a seller of purple from the city of Thyatira, who worshiped God. The Lord opened her heart to heed the things spoken by Paul" (Acts 16:14).

DATA

> Indium is a soft, silvery-white metal. It is so soft it can be used like chalk to mark other objects.

> Indium was discovered by the German chemists Ferdinand Reich and Theodor Hieronymus Richter in 1863.

> Indium has the appearance of aluminum but feels like tin.

> Indium is produced as a by-product of zinc manufacturing.

ANALYSIS

One of the most useful tools in chemistry is called the spectroscope. When substances, especially metals, are heated, they produce colored light. Each element has its own distinctive color. For example, sodium produces a yellow glow. Some other common colors are green for copper, lavender for potassium, and, of course, red for iron. (That's where we get the expression "red hot.")

There are several metals that produce similar shades of red, such as lithium, strontium, and iron. To help distinguish among these metals, the red light can be examined with the aid of a spectroscope. A prism in the spectroscope breaks the light into thin lines of color separated by dark spaces. The pattern of colored lines and dark spaces is referred to as the element's spectrum. Each element's spectrum is unique and can be used to differentiate between elements that produce similar flames. Also, the spectrum produced by heating a sample containing two or more elements can be examined to determine the individual elements in the sample.

When the German chemist Ferdinand Reich believed he had discovered a new element in 1863, he wanted to use spectroscopic analysis to verify it. He was a very capable scientist who was quite familiar with the technique. There was only one problem. Reich was color-blind. So he had to employ the services of a fellow chemist named Hieronymus Richter. The flame color produced by Reich's suspected new element was a beautiful purple that was different from any other element that had been discovered by that time. When viewed through a spectroscope, the light looked like a bright purple thread. They decided to name the element "indium," based on the Latin word *indicum*, which was a dye that the Romans used to make garments of purple. Today we call that dye (and the color it creates) indigo.

INDIGO IN BIBLE TIMES

The purple dye, indigo, was imported from Phoenicia, and it was made by removing a small gland from certain mollusks. When crushed, this gland produced a small amount of purplish fluid, which could be collected and used to dye fabrics. The scarcity of indigo made it very expensive. In Jesus' time, only the rich had purple garments. It was considered to be a mark of royalty. Even to have a few purple threads to weave into a garment was a luxury. In the parable of the rich man and Lazarus, Jesus describes the rich man as being "clothed in purple and fine linen" (Luke 16:19).

Acts chapter 16 tells the story of a Greek woman named Lydia, who is called "a seller of purple." As you might suspect, as a merchant selling such a rich fabric, Lydia was quite well to do. She owned her own home and had many servants. The Bible said that although Lydia was Greek, she "worshiped God." When she heard Paul preaching in her hometown, she was touched by the Holy Spirit and became Paul's first convert in Europe (Acts 16:13–15). Later, Lydia's home became one of the first churches (Acts 16:40).

Lydia's money, influence, and support of Paul's ministry must have been very important to the spread of the gospel in the Church's early years. Like Lydia, every Christian needs to do his or her part to support the Church and spread the gospel of Christ.

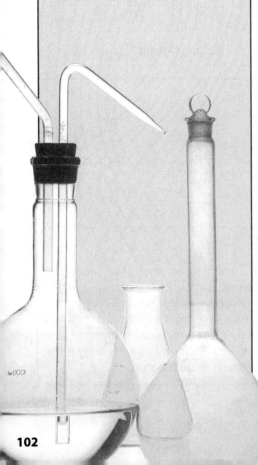

REACTION: *PURPLE, THE COLOR OF ROYALTY*

And the soldiers twisted a crown of thorns and put it on His head, and they put on Him a purple robe (John 19:2).

Jesus was a descendant of David, the greatest king in Israel's history (Matt. 1:17; Rev. 22:16). When He was born, He was recognized as a king. The wise men from the East came seeking Him, saying, "Where is He who has been born King of the Jews? For we have seen His star in the East and have come to worship Him" (Matt. 2:2). They brought Him gifts fit for a king: gold, frankincense, and myrrh (Matt. 2:11).

When Jesus entered the city of Jerusalem for the Feast of Passover, the people welcomed Him as King: "The next day a great multitude that had come to the feast, when they heard that Jesus was coming to Jerusalem, took branches of palm trees and went out to meet Him, and cried out: 'Hosanna! Blessed is He who comes in the name of the LORD! The King of Israel!'" (John 12:12–13).

But only five days later He was arrested. Again Jesus was recognized as King, but this time only mockingly. Pilate's soldiers "twisted a crown of thorns and put it on His head." Of course, the Roman soldiers knew that Roman emperors wore purple togas as a sign of their authority. So to add to Christ's humiliation, they made Him wear a purple robe. "Then they said, 'Hail, King of the Jews!' And they struck Him with their hands" (John 19:2–3). When they crucified Jesus, they placed a sign above His head that read, "Jesus of Nazareth, The King of the Jews" (John 19:19).

But we know that Jesus' kingdom was not of this earth (John 18:36). Jesus rose on the third day and ascended to His true kingdom in heaven. Someday soon He will return, wearing not a robe and crown of mockery, but attired with crowns and robes suitable for the King of kings!

"Now I [John] saw heaven opened, and behold, a white horse. And He who sat on him was called Faithful and True, and in righteousness He judges and makes war. . . . And on His head were many crowns. . . . And He has on His robe and on His thigh a name written: KING OF KINGS AND LORD OF LORDS" (Rev. 19:11–16).

QUICK QUIZ

1. Ferdinand Reich needed help to discover indium because he was_____. (Fill in the blank.)

2. A spectroscope is a scientific instrument used to analyze substances by the colors they produce _____.

| a. when they are dissolved | b. when they are heated in a flame | c. when they are in a vacuum | d. under a microscope |

3. In Bible times, purple clothing was a sign of wealth and/or _____. (Fill in the blank.)

4. In Acts 16, a Christian woman named Lydia was called "a seller of _____."

| a. cosmetics | b. bread | c. gold | d. purple |

5. Metallic indium is _____.

| a. purple | b. golden brown | c. silvery white | d. transparent |

RESPONSE

"Great Ruler of the universe, with my words I acknowledge You as my King. Help me to acknowledge Your kingship by my actions as well. Thank You for the blessing and honor of knowing You, both as king and friend. Amen."

Sn

50

118.71

TIN: "The Key to the Bronze Age"

"Tarshish was your merchant because of your many luxury goods. They gave you silver, iron, tin, and lead for your goods" (Ezek. 27:12).

DATA

> Tin is one of seven metals known from antiquity (with gold, silver, iron, copper, lead, and mercury).

> "Tin" is an old Anglo-Saxon word. The symbol Sn is from the Latin word for tin, *stannum*.

> Tin is silvery white, soft, malleable, and ductile.

> Tin was once used to make bowls, cups, eating utensils, and tinfoil (before aluminum was available). So-called tin cans are actually steel covered with a layer of tin to prevent corrosion.

> Tin is too soft to use for weapons or tools, but when combined with copper (about 80 percent copper and 20 percent tin), it becomes bronze, an alloy that is stronger than either copper or tin.

ANALYSIS

Tin is mentioned five times in the King James Version of the Bible. In Numbers 31:22, it is mentioned as one of the six metals used by the Israelites, along with gold, silver, bronze, iron, and lead. In Ezekiel 27:12, it is listed as a "luxury." Elsewhere, tin is mentioned as an impurity in the purification of silver (Isa. 1:25 and Ezek. 22:18–20).

Of course, tin's most significant use in the Bible is as a component of bronze (which the King James Version calls "brass"). For an extensive discussion of bronze in the Bible, see element 29, copper.

COINAGE IN THE BIBLE

Israel was situated in a crossroads in the Middle East and throughout their history, Israelites used a lot of different coins. At various times they were ruled by foreign conquerors, so they often used coins of other nations, including the Babylonians, Persians, Romans, and Greeks. But at times, the Jews also minted their own money.

Foreign coins often had images of pagan gods or foreign rulers. Jesus himself referred to a coin with Caesar's image in Luke 20:25. ("Render therefore to Caesar the things that are Caesar's, and to God the things that are God's.") Of course, the Israelites were prohibited from making any such images (see Exod. 20:4). Jewish coins often featured symbols of prosperity, such as fruit trees, or weapons.

The most mentioned coin in the Bible is the Roman denarius, a silver coin that Christ often used in His sermons. The denarius was the coin the Good Samaritan used (Luke 10:35). It was worth about one day's wage. Most other coins were silver also, such the Greek drachma. There were gold coins, too, but they were usually issued for special occasions and were less common.

THE WIDOW'S MITE

The least valuable coin in Israel was known by the Greek name *lepton*. It was a tiny bronze coin, smaller than a penny. Leptons that have survived to this day are usually in poor condition due to the inferior quality of metal used. The lepton really was the "penny" of the Bible. We know this coin as the "mite," from the King James translation of Jesus' observation about a widow's gift to the temple in Jerusalem.

Jesus watched as rich men gave great sums to the temple treasury. Then a poor, pious widow gave two tiny coins. Jesus was touched by her act, and He called for His disciples. He told them that, despite her poverty, she had given more to the work of God than all the others, for "she out of her poverty put in all that she had." To Jesus, who looked on the woman's heart, the "widow's mites" made of copper and tin were worth more than all of the gold and silver in the treasury (Mark 12:41–44).

REACTION: *THE WIDOWS MITES*

Then one poor widow came and threw in two mites . . . . So [Jesus] called His disciples to Himself and said to them, "Assuredly I say to you that this poor widow has put in more than all those who have given to the treasury (Mark 12:42–43).

Have you impressed God lately? Have you made Him sit up and take notice today?

This may seem like a silly question, even an irreverent one. How can we, as mere humans, impress God? He made us. He knows us for all of our good works and all of our shortcomings. He knows how many hairs are on each of our heads (Luke 12:7). We are sinners who all come woefully short of God's holiness. How could we ever do anything to impress God?

But what does Mark chapter 12 teach us? Throughout the day, Christ had watched a parade of rich men go into the temple, giving "out of their abundance." Perhaps some of them had come in with trumpets blowing, as Jesus described in Matthew 6:2. Some of these wealthy people were there for the attention, but Jesus wasn't impressed.

But the widow's meager gift of two of the smallest coins in Israel drew the Lord's attention. He did not have to craft a parable. He did not need to argue or convince. He just called His disciples together and said, "See. This is what I've been talking about. This is what you were created for. This is the Kingdom."

> Her gift was generous. Jesus said she gave "her whole livelihood."

> Her gift showed her faithfulness to God. Despite her poverty, she supported the temple of her faith.

> Her gift showed her trust in God. She had enough faith to believe that God would provide for her needs.

Have you impressed God lately?

QUICK QUIZ

1. The alloy of copper and tin is known as _____.

   a. steel   b. bronze   c. monel   d. chromium

2. The most common coin mentioned in the Bible (the denarius) was made of which element?

   a. tin   b. gold   c. silver   d. iron

3. TRUE or FALSE: Tin is a hard metal.

4. In the Parable of the Widow's Mites (in Mark 12), Jesus said the offering the widow made to the temple_____.

   a. was not worth much   b. should be given back to her   c. was worth more than all the money in the temple   d. was 10 percent of her income

5. The "widow's mite" or "lepton" could be considered the _____ of the Bible.

   a. penny   b. quarter   c. dollar   d. counterfeit money

RESPONSE

The generosity of this anonymous woman has served as an inspiration throughout the history of the Church. Just imagine meeting her someday in heaven, "crowned with a crown of righteousness" in a city where the streets are made of gold. Just imagine Jesus saying, "See, this is that lady I was telling you about."

"Lord, may I, like the widow in Your Word, ever be faithful to You. Let me not forget to worship You and support the spread of the gospel through my own efforts and with the money that I give. Help me to be generous, like the widow. In Jesus' name. Amen."

EXPERIMENT: The Electrolysis of Water

Materials:

- Connecting wires with alligator clips (Packages of 10 or so can be purchased from Radio Shack or other electronics stores for less than $10.00.)
- Glass container (one- to two-cup Pyrex measuring cup recommended)
- 9-volt batteries: 3 or 4 (the type of battery used in a smoke detector)
- Leads for mechanical pencils: 2 (The thicker, the better. Available from office supply store or art supply store. We will refer to these leads as "electrodes" in the following experiment.)
- Cloth tape or other water-resistant adhesive tape

Procedure:

1. Carefully tape the electrodes (pencil leads) to the inside of the glass cup. The bottom tips of the electrodes should be about one inch apart (2.5 cm) and about one inch from the bottom of the glass.

2. Connect the 9-volt batteries together in a series using the connecting wires. Make sure the batteries are connected properly, with the positive post of one battery connected to the negative post of the next. (The positive and negatives posts are indicated with + and – signs on the batteries. See illustration.)

3. Fill the glass cup with about two to three inches of water to cover the end of the electrodes (pencil leads).

4. Clip the free ends of the wires to the electrodes.

Observations:

1. Watch the submerged ends of the electrodes. What do you observe?

2. You should see two tiny streams of fine bubbles being generated at each electrode. The bubbles generated at the positive electrode are bubbles of oxygen. The bubbles generated at the negative electrode are hydrogen. (If the streams of bubbles do not readily form, try adding a small pinch of table salt to the water to increase its electrical conductivity.)

Where do these bubbles come from?

This experiment requires adult supervision. It has been specifically designed for educational purposes, with materials that are readily available. At its conclusion, please appropriately dispose of any by-products or food items included in the experiment.

Four 9-volt batteries connected in series will generate a voltage of 36 volts. This voltage is enough to generate a small current of electricity to travel through the water. The current causes some of the molecules of water to break apart. This process is called electrolysis.

The chemical equation used to illustrate this reaction is shown below:

$$2\,H_2O \rightarrow 2\,H_2 + O_2$$

Using electrolysis, you were able to generate pure oxygen gas (O_2) and hydrogen gas (H_2) from water! And if you carefully observe the electrodes, you should see about twice as much gas generated at the negative electrode (hydrogen) compared to the positive electrode (oxygen). (Adding a small drop of dishwashing liquid to the water helps to show the comparative amounts at each electrode.) This is reflected in the chemical equation above, which shows that two hydrogen molecules are generated for each oxygen molecule.

Electrolysis Notes:

1. Connecting more than four 9-volt batteries in series is not recommended due to the risk of painful electric shock.

2. Pencil "leads" are not really made out of lead. Pencil leads are graphite, a form of carbon. Graphite is a good conductor of electricity. (Wooden pencils, sharpened on both ends, can be used as electrodes in these experiments, if mechanical pencil leads are not available. Connect the alligator clip to the exposed pencil lead.)

Notes:

_____

_____

_____

_____

_____

_____

_____

_____

_____

_____

LET'S TAKE IT FURTHER:

Carefully disconnect the clips from the electrodes. Pour out the water.

Now you are ready to try electrolysis on other chemical compounds.

For this phase of the experiment, you will need the following:

- Hydrogen peroxide (3 percent solution in water)
- Carbonated soft drink

ALTERNATIVE 1: Hydrogen Peroxide Solution

1. Carefully pour hydrogen peroxide solution in jar.

2. Reconnect electrodes.

In this experiment, you should see bubbles generated only at the positive electrode. Why is this? What are these bubbles?

Discussion:

Hydrogen peroxide molecules are similar to water molecules, but hydrogen peroxide has one "extra" oxygen atom. See the illustration below:

Water (H_2O): H – O – H

Hydrogen peroxide (H_2O_2): H – O – O – H

This "extra" oxygen atom makes the hydrogen peroxide molecule "less stable" than water.

The hydrogen peroxide used in this experiment is actually a mixture or solution of hydrogen peroxide (3 percent) dissolved in water (97 percent).

Since it is less stable than water, the hydrogen peroxide is more easily affected by the electric current. So when an electric current is applied to a solution of hydrogen peroxide in water, the current affects the hydrogen peroxide before the water.

Electrolysis causes hydrogen peroxide, H_2O_2, to split apart, but it immediately recombines to form the more stable molecule, water, or H_2O. This leaves a free, uncombined atom of oxygen (O), which will rapidly combine with another nearby oxygen atom to form a diatomic molecule of oxygen, O_2, according to the following equation.

$2\,H_2O_2$ → $2\,H_2O + O_2$ or

H–O–O–H + H–O–O–H → H–O–H + H–O–H + O=O.

Unlike the electrolysis of water, only oxygen is formed, so only one electrode generates bubbles. This will continue until all of the hydrogen peroxide is used up and only water is left. Then two streams of bubbles will start to form as in the first part of this experiment.

This experiment requires adult supervision. It has been specifically designed for educational purposes, with materials that are readily available. At its conclusion, please appropriately dispose of any by-products or food items included in the experiment.

ALTERNATIVE 2: Carbonated Soft Drink

1. Pour out liquid from previous experiment and rinse.

2. Gently pour carbonated soft drink into cup. (Try not to make it fizz.)

3. Reconnect electrodes.

In this experiment, you should see a significant quantity of bubbles generated at the negative electrode. These bubbles are mainly a different gas: carbon dioxide.

Discussion:

Carbonated drinks (also called "pop" or "soda") are made by injecting carbon dioxide gas into sweetened flavored water. The carbon dioxide (CO_2) reacts with the water (H_2O) in the drink to form carbonic acid (H_2CO_3). This acid gives soda drinks their acidic taste and their "fizz." The reaction is:

$$H_2O + CO_2 \rightarrow H_2CO_3.$$

Electrolysis reverses this reaction.

$$H_2CO_3 \rightarrow H_2O + CO_2 \text{ (gas)}$$

As a result, carbon dioxide is produced at the negative electrode. Since carbon dioxide is a gas, it forms bubbles, which rise to the surface.

(NOTE: Of course, you don't need electricity to generate carbon dioxide from a carbonated beverage. Warm it up . . . shake it up . . . or just drink it! The "belch" you may experience after drinking soda is just the carbon dioxide being released from your stomach!)

> *You visit the earth and water it, You greatly enrich it;*
> *the river of God is full of water (Ps. 65:9).*

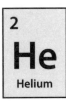

2
He
Helium

EXPERIMENT: Displacement of Helium

Materials:

- Helium balloon
- Moving vehicle

Tie the string of a helium-filled balloon securely in your car.

What will happen when your car comes to a rapid stop?

Observation:

Observe the behavior of a helium-filled balloon in a decelerating vehicle.

When you come to a stop, you may have to brace yourself to keep your body from going forward in your car. Likewise, any object in your vehicle may move toward the front.

And when your vehicle accelerates rapidly, your body is forced into your seat.

But helium balloons behave just the opposite.

As your vehicle decelerates rapidly, unlike everything else inside, the helium balloon will drift to the rear. (The phenomenon only occurs with the windows and vents closed.)

Deceleration forces the air inside the vehicle to the front, just like the people and objects in the car. But helium is lighter than air so it is displaced by the heavier moving air and drifts toward the rear.

> *"The wind blows where it wishes, and you hear the sound of it,*
> *but cannot tell where it comes from and where it goes.*
> *So is everyone who is born of the Spirit"* (John 3:8).

This experiment requires adult supervision. It has been specifically designed for educational purposes, with materials that are readily available. At its conclusion, please appropriately dispose of any by-products or food items included in the experiment.

Notes:

5
B
Boron

EXPERIMENT: Using Borax to Make Slime

Materials:

• Borax laundry conditioner

• Four-ounce bottle of white glue, such as Elmer's glue (Most so-called school glues don't work well in this experiment.)

• Water

• Food coloring (optional)

• Two bowls or large measuring cups

Procedure:

1. Pour four ounces of glue into bowl.

2. Fill empty glue bottle with water. Add water to bowl.

3. At this point, add food coloring, unless you want your slime to be white. (A teaspoon of food coloring should be about right, but you can use more or less.)

4. Mix the glue, water, and food coloring mixture thoroughly.

5. In a separate container, stir one teaspoon of borax into one cup of water.

6. Slowly pour the diluted glue into the bowl containing the borax solution.

7. Reach into the bowl and remove the mass of "slime." Don't worry about the excess water in the bowl.

8. Knead the slime slowly with your hands to make it firmer.

9. Play with your gooey creation. (Note: Afterward, store your slime in a resealable sandwich bag in your refrigerator, to keep it from going bad.)

Discussion:

How does borax create slime?

The chemical formula for borax is $Na_2B_4O_7$. Glue is a collection of long, stringy, and sticky molecules mixed with water. The borax molecules connect the glue molecules together into a "mesh" or "network" that holds water molecules inside like a sponge. The borax keeps the glue from sticking to your skin, and the water, trapped inside the network, makes the slime feel wet.

This experiment requires adult supervision. It has been specifically designed for educational purposes, with materials that are readily available. At its conclusion, please appropriately dispose of any by-products or food items included in the experiment.

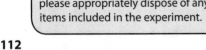

LET'S TAKE IT FURTHER:

Try these modifications:

1. Add more water to the glue.

2. Add less water to the glue or none at all.

3. Try mixing more borax into the slime.

4. Substitute blue gel glue (available from drug stores) instead of white glue.

Slime Storage Notes:

After a while, your slime may develop dark blotches or smell funny. If this happens, it is time to throw your slime away. (You can always make more!)

> *"And when she could not longer hide him, she took for him an ark of bulrushes, and daubed it with slime and with pitch, and put the child therein"* (Exod. 2:3).
> (From the story of Moses in the King James Version)

Notes:

_____

_____

_____

_____

_____

_____

_____

_____

_____

_____

_____

_____

_____

_____

_____

_____

_____

_____

6
C
Carbon

8
O
Oxygen

EXPERIMENT: Generating Carbon Dioxide

(SAFETY NOTE: This experiment involves the use of matches or a lighter and a lighted candle. It should ONLY be done under adult supervision.)

Materials:

- Baking soda (bicarbonate of soda, such as Arm and Hammer)
- Vinegar
- Large measuring cup (two- or four-cup size)
- Candle
- Lighter or matches

Procedure:

1. Place several tablespoons of baking soda in the measuring cup.

2. Pour several ounces of vinegar over the baking soda.

3. Light the candle.

4. Carefully pick up the measuring cup and tip it as if you were going to pour a liquid over the candle.

5. Observe the candle flame.

Discussion:

What happened to the candle's flame?

Vinegar contains a fairly mild acid (called acetic acid) dissolved in water. When vinegar and baking soda (sodium bicarbonate) are mixed, they generate carbon dioxide according to the following reaction:

Vinegar (acetic acid): CH_3COOH
Baking soda (sodium bicarbonate): $NaHCO_3$

$$CH_3COOH + NaHCO_3. \rightarrow CH_3COONa + H_2O + CO_2(gas)$$

Since carbon dioxide is heavier than air, it remains inside the measuring cup. When you tip the cup, the carbon dioxide gas flows from the spout of the measuring cup and downward toward the lighted candle. When it reaches the candle, the carbon dioxide engulfs the flame, blocking out the oxygen. With no oxygen, the flame goes out.

This experiment requires adult supervision. It has been specifically designed for educational purposes, with materials that are readily available. At its conclusion, please appropriately dispose of any by-products or food items included in the experiment.

LET'S TAKE IT FURTHER:

Another way to generate carbon dioxide at home is to use a carbonated beverage. Take a fresh two-liter bottle of carbonated soft drink and pour about half of it down the drain. Gently shake the bottle with your thumb held lightly over the opening. (This should be done outdoors to avoid spraying the soft drink in your house.) When the foam settles down, the upper portion of the bottle should be full of carbon dioxide released from the beverage.

Tip the bottle so that the opening is over a lighted candle. Gently squeeze the bottle to force out the carbon dioxide to snuff out the flame.

> *Like one who takes away a garment in cold weather, and like vinegar on soda, is one who sings songs to a heavy heart (Prov. 25:20).*

Notes:

EXPERIMENT: Fluoride Protection

Materials:

- Three or more raw eggs
- One bottle of fluoride dental rinse
- Vinegar

Procedure:

1. Put one raw egg in a sealable container, such as Tupperware. Fill the container with enough fluoride dental rinse to cover the egg. Leave egg in container for around 24 hours.

2. After 24 hours, remove egg and dry it off. Then mark this egg with an F (for fluoride) with a permanent marker.

3. Next take the egg marked with the F, along with two additional eggs, and put them in a 2-quart container. Fill the container with vinegar. Cover the container with a lid or cling wrap. Leave all three eggs in container for about 12 to 24 hours. You should notice the formation of bubbles around the eggs.

4. Carefully, using a large spoon, periodically remove and inspect the eggs as they soak in vinegar. What do you observe?

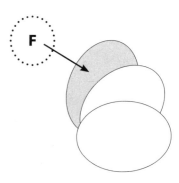

Observation:

The shells of the two eggs not marked with an F should begin to soften. The egg that is marked with an F may soften as well, but it should be noticeably harder than the other two eggs. What is happening to these eggs?

Explanation:

The hard shell of an egg is made of two components. A thin, rubbery membrane surrounds the white of the egg. This membrane is impregnated with a hard chemical called calcium carbonate (or $CaCO_3$), which gives the shell its strength. But calcium carbonate dissolves easily in acids. So when you leave an egg submerged in vinegar (which is an acid but a fairly weak one) it slowly dissolves away the calcium carbonate, weakening the egg.

The fluoride dental rinse contains a chemical called sodium fluoride (NaF). By soaking one of the eggs in it, calcium in the eggshell combined with some of the fluoride to form a material called fluoro-apatite, which is acid resistant and it protected this egg from the softening caused by the acetic acid (vinegar).

Health Note:

Fluoride has a similar protective effect on your teeth. That's why fluoride is added to toothpaste and drinking water. Fluoride is very effective in strengthening the enamel of your teeth and reducing cavities. Bacteria that live inside your mouth produce the acids that cause cavities.

This experiment requires adult supervision. It has been specifically designed for educational purposes, with materials that are readily available. At its conclusion, please appropriately dispose of any by-products or food items included in the experiment.

LET'S TAKE IT FURTHER:

Have you ever seen a "naked egg"?

For this demonstration, using a large slotted spoon, carefully remove the softened eggs with partially dissolved shells from the vinegar. Pour out the old vinegar, and cover the eggs with fresh vinegar. After 12 to 24 more hours, you will have a naked egg.

Again carefully spoon out the eggs. Now you can hold them in your hand. Rinse off any residue in the sink. You should have a plump little rubbery ball of raw egg. The membrane of the egg should be translucent and you should be able to see the yolk of the egg floating inside. You can even squeeze it slightly, but not too hard, because it might burst.

You can even put the eggs in a bowl with a little water and few drops of food coloring and color your naked eggs.

OSMOSIS:

You can use your naked eggs to study osmosis, which is the movement of water through a membrane.

Take two naked eggs. Place one overnight in a glass of corn syrup and place the other in a glass of water. (The glasses containing the eggs should be refrigerated to keep the eggs from getting rotten.) The next day, check on the eggs.

The egg that was in the water should be plump and firm, but the egg kept in the corn syrup will be shriveled and limp. This is due to osmosis.

Water molecules are small and they easily pass from the water through the egg's membrane, but the contents of the eggs (the egg white and yolk) are absorbent and they tend to "hold on" to the water that passes through, keeping it plump.

The sugar molecules in the corn syrup are too large to pass into the egg through the membrane, but water molecules that pass out of the egg are "held on" to by the corn syrup, causing the egg to shrivel. (You can reverse the process by putting the shriveled egg in a glass of water for a while.)

> *As vinegar to the teeth and smoke to the eyes,*
> *so is the lazy man to those who send him* (Prov. 10:26).

Notes:

_____

_____

_____

_____

_____

_____

_____

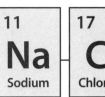 **EXPERIMENT**: Generation of Chlorine Gas by Electrolysis

11
Na
Sodium

17
Cl
Chlorine

Materials (similar to previous experiment for hydrogen):

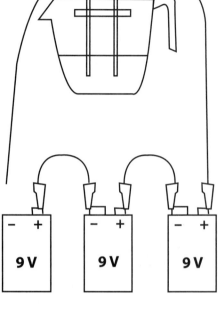

- Connecting wires with alligator clips (Packages of 10 or so can be purchased from Radio Shack or other electronics stores for less than $10.00.)
- Glass container (one- or two-cup Pyrex measuring cup recommended)
- 9-volt batteries: 3 or 4 (the type of battery used in a smoke detector)
- Leads for mechanical pencils: 2 (The thicker, the better. Available from office supply store or art supply store. We will refer to these leads as "electrodes" in the following experiment.)
- Cloth tape or other water-resistant adhesive tape
- 1 cup of liquid chlorine bleach
- Table salt

Procedure:

1. Carefully tape the electrodes (pencil leads) to the inside of the glass cup. The bottom tips of the electrodes should be about one inch apart (2.5 cm) and about one inch from the bottom of the glass.

2. Connect the 9-volt batteries together in a series using the connecting wires. Make sure the batteries are connected properly, with the positive post of one battery connected to the negative post of the next. (The positive and negatives posts should be indicated with + and – signs on the batteries. See illustration.)

3. Carefully fill the glass cup with about two to three inches of chorine bleach to cover the end of the electrodes (pencil leads). **(NOTE: Bleach may discolor fabrics and surfaces, so this experiment should only be done under adult supervision.)**

4. Connect the free ends of the wires to the electrodes.

Observations:

1. Watch the submerged ends of the electrodes. What do you observe?

2. You should see a tiny stream of fine bubbles being generated at one of the two electrodes. Carefully sniff the liquid. What do you smell?

The bubbles generated in this experiment are chlorine gas (Cl_2). As the electricity generated by the batteries passes through the liquid bleach, the current causes the dissolved chlorine in the bleach to form gaseous chlorine, by electrolysis.

This experiment requires adult supervision. It has been specifically designed for educational purposes, with materials that are readily available. At its conclusion, please appropriately dispose of any by-products or food items included in the experiment.

Electrolysis Notes:

1. Connecting more than four 9-volt batteries in series is not recommended due to the risk of painful electric shock.
2. Pencil "leads" are not really made out of lead. Pencil leads are graphite, a form of carbon. Graphite is a good conductor of electricity. (Wooden pencils, sharpened on both ends, can be used as electrodes in these experiments, if mechanical pencil leads are not available. Connect the alligator clip to the exposed pencil lead.)

LET'S TAKE IT FURTHER:

Carefully disconnect the clips from the electrodes. Pour the bleach down the sink, using plenty of water from the faucet to dilute it.

Now put several tablespoons of table salt into a separate glass. Then fill the glass about halfway with very hot tap water. With a spoon, vigorously stir the salt and water in the glass for a minute or so to dissolve the salt. (Don't worry if not all of the salt dissolves.)

Next, pour the salt mixture into the empty measuring cup. Reconnect the batteries to the electrodes. Observe what happens.

Once again, you should notice the "bleach-like" smell of chlorine gas being generated by electrolysis. In this case, the chlorine comes from the dissolved table salt, by the following reaction. (Remember: the chemical formula for table salt is sodium chloride or NaCl.)

$$2NaCl + 2H_2O \rightarrow 2NaOH + H_2 \text{ (gas)} + Cl_2 \text{ (gas)}$$

In this experiment, both hydrogen gas, H_2 (at the negative electrode), and chlorine gas, Cl_2 (at the positive electrode), are generated. However, since hydrogen is odorless, the only thing you will smell is chlorine. (Sodium hydroxide, NaOH, is also produced, but it remains dissolved in the water.)

Discussion:

This experiment gives you an idea of the way chlorine gas is manufactured on a large scale for industrial use. In many areas of the world, extremely large deposits of pure salt (NaCl) are found. For example, some salt beds are like deserts with salt crystals instead of sand.

Chlorine manufacturers first bore holes into salt beds, and then water is pumped into the holes. Then a powerful electric current is applied to the salty water. The result is large quantities of chlorine gas, which are stored under pressure in large metal cylinders. These chlorine cylinders are then sold to industry for the manufacture of plastics, solvents, and bleach. About 20 percent of all chlorine produced is used for water purification.

The by-product of this process, sodium hydroxide (or NaOH), is also valuable. It is an important chemical in industry, which is often referred to as "caustic soda."

Notes:

| 20 |
| Ca |
| Calcium |

EXPERIMENT: Study of Calcium and Collagen in Bones

To support the weight of your body, your bones must be strong. But to react to impacts and stresses without breaking, your bones have to be flexible. Fortunately, we have a wise Creator who designed our bones to satisfy both requirements. This activity will examine how bones can be strong yet flexible.

Materials:

- Several chicken leg bones
- Vinegar

Procedure:

1. Take one of the chicken bones and soak it overnight in vinegar.

2. Take another chicken bone and heat it in an oven (300–400°F) for about a half hour.

3. Then compare these two bones with a bone that hasn't been baked or soaked. How do these bones compare?

Observations:

You should notice that the vinegar soaked bone is soft and floppy, yet tough like rubber. The baked bone is hard but brittle. You can easily snap it. The original bones are flexible and strong.

Discussion:

Chicken bones, like our own bones, are made of a composite of two materials. A tough but elastic protein called collagen forms the basic structure of the bone. The collagen framework is strengthened by a hard chemical called calcium phosphate.

This experiment requires adult supervision. It has been specifically designed for educational purposes, with materials that are readily available. At its conclusion, please appropriately dispose of any by-products or food items included in the experiment.

Soaking the bone in vinegar caused the calcium phosphate to dissolve, which took away the bone's stiffness, leaving the rubbery collagen behind. (Vinegar is a weak acid that dissolves calcium compounds, but not most organic compounds such as proteins.)

Heating the other bone destroyed the collagen but left the calcium mineral behind. About half of the weight of your bones is made up of calcium phosphate.

Have mercy on me, O LORD, for I am weak;
O LORD, heal me, for my bones are troubled (Ps. 6:2).

Notes:

26
Fe
Iron

EXPERIMENT: Finding Iron Particles in Your Nutritious Breakfast Cereal

Materials:

- One cup of iron-fortified flaked breakfast cereal, such as Total (Nutrition information on box should say "100 percent of daily requirement" for iron.)
- Gallon-sized plastic food storage bag
- Rolling pin
- Strong magnet
- 8-1/2 x 11 sheet of white paper

Procedure:

1. Put the cereal in the plastic bag and lay it on a flat surface such as a kitchen cutting board.

2. Roll the rolling pin back and forth over the cereal in the bag, until the cereal is crushed into a coarse powder.

3. Place about a tablespoon of the crushed cereal onto the piece of paper.

4. Hold the magnet under the paper and move it in a circular motion under the cereal. What do you observe?

Observations:

You should see tiny pieces of the cereal being dragged around by the magnet under the paper. Each of these little bits is actually a tiny piece of iron coated with cereal. You may see black specks attracted by the magnet as well. These are tiny iron particles without a cereal coating.

Discussion:

It may seem strange to think that you are eating tiny pieces of iron for breakfast, but adding iron particles to cereal mix before it is dried and made into flakes is an inexpensive and effective way of adding nutrition to your cereal.

> *For behold, I have made you this day*
> *a fortified city and an iron pillar* (Jer. 1:18).

Notes:

28 Ni Nickel

29 Cu Copper

EXPERIMENT: Using Electroplating to Coat a Quarter with a Thin Layer of Copper

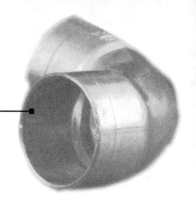

Materials:

- Connecting wires with alligator clips (Packages of 10 or so can be purchased from Radio Shack or other electronics stores for less than $10.00.)
- Glass container (one- to two-cup Pyrex measuring cup recommended)
- One 9-volt battery (the type of battery used in a smoke detector)
- A small piece of copper (for example, a half-inch copper "elbow" from the plumbing section of a hardware store)
- Vinegar
- Cloth tape or other water-resistant adhesive tape (The sticky part of a Band-Aid works well.)

Procedure:

1. Pour about one-half inch of vinegar into the glass.

2. Attach one alligator clip to the piece of copper and let it rest on the bottom of the glass. It will be only partially submerged in the vinegar. Tape the wire to the side of the glass. Attach the other end of the wire to the positive (+) pole of the 9-volt battery.

3. Take another connecting wire and clip one end to a quarter. Suspend the quarter, with about one half of it submerged in the vinegar. Tape the wire to the side of the glass so that the quarter and the piece of copper are about one-half inch apart. Now connect the other clip to the negative (-) pole of the battery.

4. If you see small bubbles start to form on the quarter within about a minute, then you have set up your experiment properly.

5. This experiment should take 30 minutes to an hour. Afterward, pour the vinegar down the drain and wash the glass thoroughly before re-use.

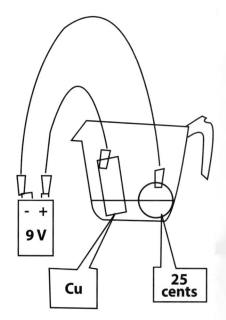

Observations:

1. The bubbles that form on the quarter are bubbles of carbon dioxide caused by the flow of electricity through the vinegar.

2. Within several minutes, you should see the quarter getting darker. This is the start of a layer of copper being deposited on the quarter.

3. Within 20 to 30 minutes, you should notice a blue tint in the vinegar, especially near the piece of copper.

4. After 30 to 60 minutes, remove the quarter. What does it look like?

This experiment requires adult supervision. It has been specifically designed for educational purposes, with materials that are readily available. At its conclusion, please appropriately dispose of any by-products or food items included in the experiment.

Discussion:

This experiment is a simplified example of an important industrial process called "electroplating." The acidic vinegar solution causes the copper to start to dissolve. The positive electrical charge on the copper speeds up the dissolving process. When copper dissolves, it forms copper ions, which have a positive charge. Scientists use the following notation to show a copper ion: Cu^{++}. (The two plus signs indicate that each copper atom has given up two negatively charged electrons.) As more and more copper ions form, the vinegar begins to take on a bluish tinge, which is typical of copper solutions.

By connecting the quarter to the negative pole of the battery, you create a negative electrical charge on the quarter. This negative charge attracts the positive copper ions (Cu^{++}) to the quarter. When the copper ions reach the quarter, they "get back" their two "missing" electrons and turn back into metallic copper, which is deposited on the quarter.

When you remove the quarter, you should be able to wipe off most of the copper with a paper towel. This dark, sludge-like material is actually made of very small particles. Scientists would call this "finely divided" copper. Because the particles are so tiny, they appear black instead of copper's normal reddish brown color.

If you gently wipe off the black layer of copper, you should notice a brownish tint on the part of the quarter that was submerged. This is copper plating.

LET'S TAKE IT FURTHER:

Of course, several types of metals can be used for plating, but copper is fairly inexpensive and easy to see because of its unique color. Also, quarters are mostly made of nickel, which is inert. That's why the copper didn't bond to it very well.

You can try plating other metal objects with copper, such as nails, paper clips, and aluminum foil.

> *Alexander the coppersmith did me much harm.*
> *May the Lord repay him according to his works (2 Tim. 4:14).*

Notes:

40	
Zr	
Zirconium	

EXPERIMENT: Study a "Hygroscopic" Zirconium Compound.

Some compounds absorb and hold onto moisture. These compounds are called "hygroscopic." Some hygroscopic compounds attract water so strongly that they actually draw water vapor from the air. Some are so strong that if you leave them exposed to the air for very long, they actually form a puddle of liquid!

But other hygroscopic substances only absorb liquid water. One of these, called "aluminum zirconium trichlorohydrex," is the main ingredient in many antiperspirants.

Materials:

- Solid antiperspirant containing aluminum zirconium trichlorohydrex
- Aluminum foil
- Large bowl
- Water and ice

Procedure:

1. Take a sheet of aluminum foil large enough to cover the bowl. Make a mark on the foil using the deodorant stick, for example, a Z for zirconium.

2. Fill the bowl almost to the rim with ice water.

3. Cover the bowl with foil. Make sure the antiperspirant streak is facing up.

4. Observe water condensing on the aluminum foil.

Discussion:

Moisture in the air will condense on the cold aluminum foil. However, the mark that you made on the foil should appear to stay dry. This is because the zirconium compound in the antiperspirant absorbs the moisture.

When looking for a chemical to control perspiration, scientists needed a substance that was (1) hygroscopic but (2) not so hygroscopic that it absorbed moisture from the air, and (3) most of all it had to be safe for contact with skin. Aluminum zirconium trichlorohydrex turned out to be an excellent choice.

> *In the sweat of your face you shall eat bread till you return to the ground (Gen. 3:19).*

This experiment requires adult supervision. It has been specifically designed for educational purpose with materials that are readily available. At its conclusion please appropriately dispose of any by-products or food items included in the experiment.

Notes:

Quick Quiz Answers

1~Hydrogen
1. c
2. c
3. false
4. hydros
5. 90

2~Helium
1. c
2. helios
3. Sir William Ramsey
4. idolatry
5. d

3~Lithium
1. b
2. a. lithos, b. petra
3. d
4. alkali
5. foundation

4~Beryllium
1. b
2. d
3. ore
4. a
5. jewels

5~Boron
1. medicine
2. borax
3. a
4. b
5. Louis Pasteur

6~Carbon
1. The Industrial Revolution
2. methane
3. b
4. a
5. d

7~Nitrogen
1. a
2. c
3. nitrogen-fixing bacteria
4. legumes
5. b

8~Oxygen
1. c
2. d
3. ozone
4. true
5. b

9~Fluorine
1. d
2. reactive
3. b
4. the Halogen Family
5. martyrs

10~Neon
1. b
2. a
3. new
4. by letting our "light shine before men"
5. William Ramsey

11~Sodium
1. a
2. d
3. b
4. salt of the earth
5. d

12~Magnesium
1. Humphry Davy
2. d
3. laxative
4. spa
5. seven

13~Aluminum
1. c
2. Fredrick Wohler
3. d
4. the Civil War
5. praise God

14~Silicon
1. silica
2. Jons Berzulius
3. Paul
4. c
5. arenologists

15~Phosphorus
1. d
2. c
3. gold
4. fool's gold
5. it glows in the dark

16~Sulfur
1. brimstone
2. odors
3. b
4. fire and brimstone
5. a

17~Chlorine
1. halogen
2. d

3. New York
4. Lake Michigan
5. c

18~Argon
1. lazy
2. a
3. William Ramsey
4. a
5. titanium

19~Potassium
1. potash
2. c
3. b
4. dust of the earth
5. Sir Humphry Davy

20~Calcium
1. b
2. a
3. true
4. "meat" or "solid food"
5. dairy

21~Scandium
1. metallurgy
2. b
3. a
4. c
5. yeast or leaven

22~Titanium
1. d
2. d
3. b
4. b
5. minister

23~Vanadium
1. c
2. rust
3. c
4. galvanized
5. in heaven

24~Chromium
1. chroma
2. a
3. wisdom
4. the French Revolution
5. chrome plating

25~Manganese
1. c
2. d
3. a
4. steel
5. d

26~Iron
1. c
2. Egypt
3. iron oxide
4. hemoglobin
5. c

27~Cobalt
1. a
2. d
3. arsenic
4. c
5. d

28~Nickel
1. c
2. d
3. c
4. true
5. glassmakers

29~Copper
1. b
2. c
3. a
4. c
5. d

30~Zinc
1. galvanization
2. d
3. spangling
4. a
5. b

31~Gallium
1. b
2. a
3. true
4. confusion
5. false

32~Germanium
1. a
2. d
3. b
4. c
5. spontaneous generation

33~Arsenic
1. a
2. true
3. true
4. a
5. Marsh

34~Selenium
1. b
2. d
3. a

4. c
5. d

35~Bromine
1. b
2. a
3. c
4. c
5. Lazarus

36~Krypton
1. argon
2. a
3. d
4. c
5. the Nobel Prize

37~Rubidium
1. the Bunsen burner
2. a
3. a
4. the Grand Canyon
5. true

38~Strontium
1. d
2. Alessandro Volta
3. d
4. electrolysis
5. b

39~Yttrium
1. a
2. b
3. magnet
4. a
5. d

40~Zirconium
1. b
2. c
3. a
4. c
5. b

41~Niobium
1. a
2. b
3. c
4. a
5. by-product

42~Molybdenum
1 lead
2. a
3. a
4. c
5. trace

43~Technetium
1. man-made or artificial
2. d
3. d
4. a
5. fuel rods

44~ Ruthenium
1. Platinum Group
2. a
3. b
4. c
5. c

45~Rhodium
1. A catalyst is a substance that, by its presence, changes the rate of a chemical reaction without itself being consumed in the reaction.
2. a
3. true
4. b
5. the conversion of the Gentiles

46~Palladium
1. d
2. d
3. William Hyde Wollaston
4. c
5. c

47~Silver
1. b
2. b
3. c
4. a
5. c

48~Cadmium
1. c
2. a
3. b
4. heavy
5. d

49~Indium
1. colorblind
2. b
3. royalty
4. d
5. c

50~Tin
1. b
2. c
3. false
4. c
5. a

Glossary

alchemy – a pre-modern, unscientific philosophy that sought out mystical goals, such as life extension, panaceas (cures for diseases), and, especially, means to transform base substances into gold.

alkali (metal) – a group of metal elements occupying group I of the periodic table, namely lithium, sodium, potassium, rubidium, cesium, and francium. Alkali metals are soft, silvery white, low-density, low-melting point, and highly reactive.

alkaline earth (metal) – a group of metal elements occupying group 2 of the periodic table, namely beryllium, magnesium, calcium, strontium, barium, and radium. Alkaline earth metals are soft, silvery-white, low-density, low-melting point, and highly reactive, but generally less reactive than the alkali metals.

alloy – a homogenous mixture of two or more metals (and sometimes other elements, especially carbon). Alloys generally have different (often superior) properties compared to the constituent metals.

antiseptic – a technique or chemical solution used to destroy microorganisms that cause disease.

beryl – a mineral ($Be_3Al_2Si_6O_{18}$) that is the chief source of beryllium. Beryl has a hexagonal structure and is used as a gem.

boric acid – a white or clear compound (H_3BO_3) with many uses, especially as an antiseptic.

brass – an alloy of copper and zinc.

brimstone – a noxious, flammable substance, frequently referred to in the Bible and generally identified as the element sulfur.

bronze – an alloy of copper and tin

catalyst – a substance, typically used in small amounts, that modifies, usually increases, the rate of a chemical reaction without being consumed in the reaction.

columbium – an alternate name for the element niobium.

combustion – the rapid oxidation of a substance, especially a carbon-containing material, which generates light and heat.

diatomic – referring to a molecule made up of two atoms. Except for the noble gasses, elemental gasses are generally diatomic: hydrogen, oxygen, nitrogen, and the halogens.

disinfection – the destruction of disease-causing microorganisms.

electrolysis – decomposition of a chemical compound caused by the passage of an electric current.

Ephesus – an ancient Greek city, one of the most prosperous, located in Asia Minor. The site of the famous Temple of Diana.

Epsom, England – an English town where Epsom salt (magnesium sulfate) was discovered.

essential element – an element that is necessary for life and health.

fool's gold – a substance, especially iron pyrite, that miners sometimes mistake for gold.

Freon – a trademark name for any of various nonflammable fluorocarbons compounds used for refrigeration and air conditioning.

galvanization – the coating of steel or iron objects with zinc in order to prevention corrosion.

halogen – a member of group 17 of the periodic table, namely, fluorine, chlorine, bromine, iodine, or astatine. Each of the halogens has seven electrons in its outermost electron shell.

hemoglobin – the iron-containing, oxygen-transporting, red-colored protein in red blood cells.

hydrogen bond – a weak chemical bond between a hydrogen atom in one water molecule and an oxygen atom in another water molecule. This bond is roughly about 5 percent as strong a covalent bond, and it is responsible for many of water's unique physical properties. (Weaker hydrogen bonds also occur within and among in many organic molecules, and these are very important for many life processes.)

idolatry – the worship of idols. Often used to describe the sin of placing anything other than God as the first priority in one's life.

industrial revolution – a social and economic change related to great increases in the production of goods in a society, especially such a change that occurred in England, beginning in the mid-18th century.

laus Deo – a Latin phrase meaning "Praise God." The phrase appears on the pyramid-shaped, aluminum lightning arrester on the top of the Washington Monument.

leaven – yeast.

legume – any member of a family of plants that bear their seeds in pods (beans, peas, clover, etc.) and generally harbor nitrogen-fixing bacteria, in a symbiotic relationship.

metal – an element with properties such as luster, high heat and electrical conductivity, malleability, ductility, and other typical properties. Most of the elements of the periodic table are metals

metalloid – an element that has both metallic and non-metallic properties, or properties intermediate between a metal and a nonmetal, namely, boron, silicon, germanium, arsenic, antimony, tellurium, and polonium. (Carbon is also sometimes considered a metalloid.) Metalloids are also called semi-metals.

metallurgy – the study of metals and their alloys.

nitrogen-fixing bacteria – certain bacteria that are able to convert atmospheric nitrogen into nitrogen compounds that are usable by other organisms.

noble gas – a member of the family of extremely unreactive atmospheric gasses in group 18 of the periodic table, namely helium, neon, argon, krypton, xenon, or radon. Also called the inert gasses.

ozone – the triatomic form of oxygen (O_3). It is relatively unstable in the lower atmosphere, but in the upper atmosphere, ozone is more persistent and it helps to protect the earth from harmful solar radiation.

pearl – a gem that often illustrates aspects of the Kingdom of heaven in the Bible.

phosphor – a substance that emits light when it is struck by a beam of electrons. Used to illuminate television screens.

platinum group metals – a group of six metallic elements with platinum-like properties, namely, ruthenium, rhodium, palladium, osmium, iridium, and platinum.

potash – a white, translucent chemical substance (potassium carbonate, K_2CO_3) used to make glass, pigments, ceramics, soaps, and other products. (Formerly produced by the burning of hardwood trees, but now by mining.)

ruby – a deep-red, translucent form of corundum, valued as a gem. Often associated with wisdom in the Bible.

rust – iron oxide.

silica – a white or clear crystalline compound, silicon dioxide or SiO_2, occurring abundantly on the earth as quartz, sand, flint, and other important minerals.

Sparta – an ancient Greek city-state, known for its military prowess, austere culture, and superior weapons.

spectroscope – a scientific device used to analyze the optical spectrum of incandescent objects to determine their compositions. The incandescent objects may be laboratory samples or distant stars.

spontaneous generation – an unscientific and discredited belief that living organisms may develop from nonliving matter. Prior to the work of scientists such as Louis Pasteur and Dr. Joseph Lister, spontaneous generation was widely believed, even by scientists (also called abiogenesis).

Teflon – the trademark name for polytetrafluoroethylene, a long-chain fluorocarbon. It is white and waxy with a high degree of chemical inertness and low friction.

typhoid fever – an extremely contagious disease of the digestive system, spread by contaminated food or water. Typhoid fever has been virtually eliminated in the developed world due to chlorination and proper sanitation.

voltaic pile – a source of electricity consisting of alternating disks of two different metals separated by absorbent pads, moistened by an acid or other electrolyte. Named for the inventor Alessandro Volta.

welding – the joining of pieces of metal by the application of heat, sometimes using an intermediate filler metal of a lower melting point.

widow's mite – in Roman times, a coin minted by the Jews. It was made of low-quality bronze and is often referred to as the "penny of the Bible." Also called by its Greek name, the lepton.

yeast – a unicellular, benefical fungus capable of fermenting carbohydrates, responsible for the rising of bread. Also called leaven.

Index

ELEMENTS OF FAITH
P E R I O D I C   T A B L E

Group
1
IA

1
H
Hydrogen
1.00794

2
IIA

Atomic Number
Symbol
Name
Atomic Weight*

1
H
Hydrogen
1.00794

☐ **Solids**
▨ **Liquids**
▨ **Gases**
☐ **Artificially Prepared**

Period

3	4
Li	**Be**
Lithium	Beryllium
6.941	9.012182

11	12
Na	**Mg**
Sodium	Magnesium
22.989770	24.3050

3	4	5	6	7	8	9
IIIB	IVB	VB	VIB	VIIB	VIII	

19	20	21	22	23	24	25	26	27
K	**Ca**	**Sc**	**Ti**	**V**	**Cr**	**Mn**	**Fe**	**Co**
Potassium	Calcium	Scandium	Titanium	Vanadium	Chromium	Manganese	Iron	Cobalt
39.0983	40.078	44.955910	47.867	50.9415	51.9961	54.938049	55.845	58.933200

37	38	39	40	41	42	43	44	45
Rb	**Sr**	**Y**	**Zr**	**Nb**	**Mo**	**Tc**	**Ru**	**Rh**
Rubidium	Strontium	Yttrium	Zirconium	Niobium	Molybdenum	Technetium	Ruthenium	Rhodium
85.4678	87.62	88.90585	91.224	92.90638	95.94	(98)	101.07	102.90550

55	56		72	73	74	75	76	77
Cs	**Ba**		**Hf**	**Ta**	**W**	**Re**	**Os**	**Ir**
Cesium	Barium		Hafnium	Tantalum	Tungsten	Rhenium	Osmium	Iridium
132.90545	137.327		178.49	180.9479	183.84	186.207	190.23	192.217

87	88		104	105	106	107	108	109
Fr	**Ra**		**Rf**	**Db**	**Sg**	**Bh**	**Hs**	**Mt**
Francium	Radium		Rutherfordium	Dubnium	Seaborgium	Bohrium	Hassium	Meitnerium
(223)	(226)		(261)	(262)	(266)	(264)	(277)	(268)

"Of gold and silver and bronze and iron there is no limit. Arise and begin working, and the LORD be with you."

—1 Chronicles 22:16

Lanthanides

57	58	59	60	61	62
La	**Ce**	**Pr**	**Nd**	**Pm**	**Sm**
Lanthanum	Cerium	Praseodymium	Neodymium	Promethium	Samarium
138.9055	140.116	140.90765	144.24	(145)	150.36

Actinides

89	90	91	92	93	94
Ac	**Th**	**Pa**	**U**	**Np**	**Pu**
Actinium	Thorium	Protactinium	Uranium	Neptunium	Plutonium
(227)	232.0381	231.03588	238.02891	(237)	(244)

*Based upon ^{12}C. () indicates the mass number of the most stable isotope.

						18 VIIIA

2 He Helium 4.002602

13 IIIA	14 IVA	15 VA	16 VIA	17 VIIA

| 5 **B** Boron 10.811 | 6 **C** Carbon 12.0107 | 7 **N** Nitrogen 14.0067 | 8 **O** Oxygen 15.9994 | 9 **F** Fluorine 18.9984032 | 10 **Ne** Neon 20.1797 |

| 13 **Al** Aluminum 26.981538 | 14 **Si** Silicon 28.0855 | 15 **P** Phosphorus 30.973761 | 16 **S** Sulfur 32.065 | 17 **Cl** Chlorine 35.453 | 18 **Ar** Argon 39.948 |

10	11 IB	12 IIB

| 28 **Ni** Nickel 58.6934 | 29 **Cu** Copper 63.546 | 30 **Zn** Zinc 65.409 | 31 **Ga** Gallium 69.723 | 32 **Ge** Germanium 72.64 | 33 **As** Arsenic 74.92160 | 34 **Se** Selenium 78.96 | 35 **Br** Bromine 79.904 | 36 **Kr** Krypton 83.798 |

| 46 **Pd** Palladium 106.42 | 47 **Ag** Silver 107.8682 | 48 **Cd** Cadmium 112.411 | 49 **In** Indium 114.818 | 50 **Sn** Tin 118.710 | 51 **Sb** Antimony 121.760 | 52 **Te** Tellurium 127.60 | 53 **I** Iodine 126.90447 | 54 **Xe** Xenon 131.293 |

| 78 **Pt** Platinum 195.078 | 79 **Au** Gold 196.96655 | 80 **Hg** Mercury 200.59 | 81 **Tl** Thallium 204.3833 | 82 **Pb** Lead 207.2 | 83 **Bi** Bismuth 208.98038 | 84 **Po** Polonium (209) | 85 **At** Astatine (210) | 86 **Rn** Radon (222) |

| 110 **Uun** Ununnilium (281) | 111 **Uuu** Unununium (272) | 112 **Uub** Ununbium (285) | | 114 **Uuq** Ununquadium (289) | | 116 **Uuh** Ununhexium (292) | | |

| 63 **Eu** Europium 151.964 | 64 **Gd** Gadolinium 157.25 | 65 **Tb** Terbium 158.92534 | 66 **Dy** Dysprosium 162.500 | 67 **Ho** Holmium 164.93032 | 68 **Er** Erbium 167.259 | 69 **Tm** Thulium 168.93421 | 70 **Yb** Ytterbium 173.04 | 71 **Lu** Lutetium 174.967 |

| 95 **Am** Americium (243) | 96 **Cm** Curium (247) | 97 **Bk** Berkelium (247) | 98 **Cf** Californium (251) | 99 **Es** Einsteinium (252) | 100 **Fm** Fermium (257) | 101 **Md** Mendelevium (258) | 102 **No** Nobelium (259) | 103 **Lr** Lawrencium (262) |

NIST SP 966 (September 2002)
For a description of the data, visit physics.nist.gov/data

Selected Bibliography

Bryson, Bill (2005), *A Short History of Nearly Everything*, Broadway Books, New York

Ede, Andrew (2006), *The Chemical Element: A Historical Perspective,* Greenwood Publishing Group, Westport. Connecticut

Emsley, John (2001), *Nature's Building Blocks: An A-Z Guide to the Elements*, Oxford University Press, Oxford

Heiserman, David L. (1991), *Exploring Chemical Elements and Their Compounds,* McGraw-Hill, Columbus, Ohio

Morris, Richard (2003), *The Last Sorcerers: The Path from Alchemy to the Periodic Table*, Joseph Henry Press, Washington

Stwertka, Albert (2002) *A Guide to the Elements,* 2nd Ed., Oxford University Press, Oxford

Vine, W. E. et al. (1985), V*ine's Expository Dictionary of Biblical Words,* Thomas Nelson Publishers, Nashville, Tennessee

Weeks, Mary Elvira and Leicester, H. M (1968), *Discovery of the Elements*, 7th Ed., Journal of Chemical Education, Easton, Pennsylvania